# The Struggle Within:
# Prisons, Political Prisoners,

KER
SPL
EBE
DEB

2014

*The Struggle Within: Prisons, Political Prisoners,*
*and Mass Movements in the United States*

© 2014 Dan Berger
Foreword © 2014 Ruth Wilson Gilmore
Afterword © 2014 dream hampton
This edition © 2014 PM Press and Kersplebedeb

ISBN: 978-1-60486-955-2
Library of Congress Control Number: 2013956914


Kersplebedeb Publishing and Distribution
CP 63560
CCCP Van Horne
Montreal, Quebec
Canada H3W 3H8
www.kersplebedeb.com
www.leftwingbooks.net

PM Press
P.O. Box 23912
Oakland, CA 94623
www.pmpress.org


Layout by Kersplebedeb
Cover Design: John Yates

Printed in the USA by the Employee Owners of Thomson-Shore in
Dexter, Michigan
www.thomsonshore.com

*For Safiya (1950–2003)*
*& for Herman (1942–2013)*

*For Laura*
*& for Saleem*

*For those who generate,*
*imagine, and organize*
*toward freedom*

"When the prison doors are opened the real dragon will fly out."

# Contents

# Acknowledgments

A different version of the main text appeared as "The Real Dragons" in Matt Meyer, ed., *Let Freedom Ring: Documents from the Movements to Free U.S. Political Prisoners* (Oakland and Montreal: PM Press/Kersplebedeb, 2008), 3–46.

Thanks to Matt Meyer for the original volume and the push to draft the original essay, to Bob Lederer for his prodigious editing and analysis, to B. Loewe for the constant inspiration and the many years of being there at the right time, and to Robert Saleem Holbrook (www.freesalim.net) for his organizing and his encouragement to create this book.

Thanks to Ruthie Gilmore and dream hampton for their contributions, and to Laura Whitehorn and Susie Day for the good humor and endless support.

Thanks to all the people on both sides of the wall who have worked to rid the world of racial, sexual, and political repression.

Finally and always, a profound thank you to the many other friends and comrades whose vision and commitment inform my own in too many ways to enumerate.

## SAME BOAT

Back in 1972 Angela Y. Davis eloquently dismantled an interviewer's question about the United States, Black people, and violence. At the time she was in jail awaiting trial. The filmed encounter gathered dust for decades in a Swedish archive before appearing in the 2011 documentary *Black Power Mixtape*. Two things are amazing about the piece. First, that it happened; today it's nearly impossible for media to request conversations with specific prisoners in California. Second, the brilliant captive spelled out systemic violence in both general and personal terms, when someone else might have used the opportunity to insist on her own individual innocence.

Abolition's principal theorist and best-known practitioner, Professor Davis has dedicated her entire life to the global struggle against racial capitalism's relentless dispossession. In stark contrast to the former political prisoner's example, too much twenty-first century U.S.-based anti-prison advocacy huddles within a safe limit. The goal has become to find people who are relatively or absolutely innocent under the law, and agitate for their release. Make no mistake: getting people out is a good thing. But the persuasive means used to attract attention and gain sympathy often reinforces the deadly belief that aside from some errors confinement reduces more harm than it generates. This kind of thinking detours anti-prison work into a charitable enterprise—to help the so-called deserving—rather than what it should be—a cornerstone of large-scale fights for social, economic, and environmental justice.

The purpose of abolition is to expose and defeat all the relationships and policies that make the United States the world's top cop, warmonger, and jailer. Practicalities rather than metaphors determine the focus and drive the analysis, because the scope of prison touches every aspect of ordinary life. Thus, it is possible and necessary to identify all those points of contact and work from the ground up to change them. This ambition makes some people impatient, as well it should. Abolition is a movement to end systemic violence, including the interpersonal vulnerabilities and displacements that keep the system going. In other words, the goal is to change how we interact with each other and the planet by putting people before profits, welfare before warfare, and life over death.

Big problems require big solutions. Nothing happens all at once; big answers are the painstaking accumulation of smaller achievements. But dividing a problem into pieces in order to solve the whole thing is altogether different from defining a problem solely in terms of the bits that seem easiest to fix. In the first instance, the remedy for each piece must develop in relation to its effect on actual or possible remedies for the other pieces. The other way is to solve a small part without considering whether the outcome strengthens or weakens the big problem's hold on the world. In other words, there's breaking down and then there's breaking down.

The distinction sketched out above is the difference between reformist reform—tweak Armageddon—and non-reformist reform—deliberate change that does not create more obstacles in the larger struggle. Some of the timidity in the fight against warehousing humans in cages for part or all of their lives results from the lethal synthesis of abandoned optimism and calculated convenience. People think there's no alternative to capitalism, and in a weird distortion of capitalism itself, imagine all aspects of life as winners and losers in a zero-sum game. Many funders of anti-prison advocacy—whether through arrogance or anxiety—narrow the scope of what can be done with resources that pass through the tiny social-justice portfolio door. And finally, the challenge seems so enormous that many desperately conclude it's better to save the "deserving" weak (women or children or addicts) and cross their fingers that everyone else can swim on their own.

Why emphasize the social and organizational importance of thinking about the big picture for all activities great and small? Contemporary oppositional political society seems to be constantly reorganizing itself into fragments. While the assertion of particular needs, struggles, and identities must necessarily be part of the project to free ourselves, the structural effect of everyday political disintegration is fatal. It undermines the people's collective capacity powerfully and self-consciously to transform an already-existing popular front into a unified force. Such a united front would—could already!—have enough breadth and momentum to change our fate while sustaining our delightful or even irritating differences. Where life is precious life is precious, anywhere on this big fragile boat afloat across the universe.

## THE POLITICS OF PUNISHMENT

When it comes to prison, lots of people think of the Thirteenth Amendment to the U.S. Constitution as a window in time through which the hand of the past reaches and directs the present. Let's go back further. Modern prisons developed about the same time that thirteen settler colonies in North America threw off British rule to form the United States. Given the origin of the United States in Indigenous land theft and genocide, chattel slavery, and patriarchy, we know the ruling elite did not put pen to paper to guarantee liberty or equality for any but a few of the "all" indicated in the Declaration of Independence. So then we have to wonder—why did they bother with the Bill of Rights, guaranteeing due process and trials by peers, and prohibiting cruel and unusual punishment? A reasonable conclusion is that the guys in charge didn't want their political enemies to be able secretly or singularly to harm them if they should fall.

The awareness, two and a half centuries ago, that punishment could be used to expose vulnerable people *who had every advantage* to unfairness or torture—when legal, brutal, systematic inequality already guaranteed *disadvantage* for everybody else—brings us to the volume in hand. The politics of punishment has become a hot topic. Thousands of books, journals, documentaries, reports, and other materials discuss how and to what end federal, state, and local governments developed the laws, facilities, personnel, and news-grabbing rationalizations by which millions of U.S. residents—whose power and status were modest to begin with—have been arrested, charged, tried, and sentenced to prison or other punishments which often permanently hobble life in the free world. But oddly enough, the political message about contemporary mass incarceration often fails to take deep notice of the many political prisoners who are in custody because of their beliefs no less than actions of which they have been accused and convicted.

## POLITICAL PRISONERS

The habit of forgetting or ignoring political prisoners is connected with the tendency, outlined earlier—to subdivide people locked up into those who deserve to be rescued and those who don't. But it is also organized by the anti-political tendencies of reformist reform, which embrace the sentimental maxim that whatever's wrong with the United States will be fixed by what's right with it. Not so fast. The weapon of civil death suppresses the modest power and status of all people locked up. *The Struggle Within* is about those who believe hierarchies of race, gender, wealth, colonialism, and planetary exploitation will never just time out and disappear, but rather require focused effort to get rid of them. This historical fact returns us to the abolitionist imperative.

Dan Berger has thoughtfully assembled stories so that we can all understand why things happen where they do. No reader is obligated to agree with or approve of the people and movements portrayed in this book. But we equally share the responsibility to understand how and to what extent prison concentrates the relationships and vulnerabilities that aboli lion—nonrctormist reform—seeks to change.

## POSTSCRIPT

The day I completed these few words a federal judge in Louisiana overturned Herman Wallace's conviction on the grounds that women were explicitly excluded from the grand jury. Think about it. A member of the Black Panther Party for Self-Defense, Wallace died a free man three days later. He had been put in solitary confinement at about the same time Angela Y. Davis was interviewed in Marin County Jail. There are others doing life in the hole: some are in old-fashioned fetid cages like the one where Wallace was. Others are in ultramodern mechanized dungeons like those in California's Pelican Bay State Prison, whence the hunger strikes of the past two years have arisen to end the international human rights violation—torture—that solitary confinement is recognized to be. Whatever beliefs they had when sent to prison, the hunger strikers have developed a political understanding of the conditions in which they live—and in so doing have reached out to end "hostilities among the races" in the free world as a necessary context for liberating themselves.

Dan Berger's book presents a view into the deepest recesses of walls and cages. As you read remember that individuals like Nelson Mandela and Harriet Tubman, whose motives and justifications people today do not recoil from, were not framed; they did it. Freedom Now.

Elspeth Meyer

# Introduction

POLITICAL PRISONERS OCCUPY A CRUCIAL POSITION IN FREEDOM MOVEMENTS AROUND THE WORLD; their incarceration signals the terror of state repression, and their activism defines the principled, long-term commitments of our movements. Working for their full freedom constitutes a vital element in building, defending, and sustaining the revolutionary traditions for which they have fought. In ways political and personal, fighting for their release grounds radicalism in its layered history: it puts long-term activists who have borne the brunt of repression in public view, connects younger radicals with older generations, and, in the West, exposes the contradictions of liberal democracy. As such, freeing political prisoners always achieves a giant victory for the Left, just as work on their behalf offers much-needed opportunities to learn from the strengths and weaknesses of previous struggles and to build coalition among the many communities in struggle. Political prisoner campaigns can provide the chance to improve people's material conditions, to free people from the state's clutches before medical neglect, long sentences, or open execution can take their lives. They also enable us, ideally, to build on the best of those traditions while avoiding some of their pitfalls.

The connection to movement history generated by working to free political prisoners is multifaceted: just as participation in the struggle expands one's knowledge of history, so too is our organizing strengthened through at least a provisional awareness of the movements and conditions, ideologies and strategies, that produced the revolutionaries who have served or are now serving time in American gulags. What follows is a brief history of some of the key cases, political ideas, and social movements out of which U.S. political prisoners have come in the past five decades.

The state uses the imprisonment of political leaders and rank-and-file activists as a bludgeon against movement victo-

ries. Their incarceration is a reminder of the strength, potential, and, just as crucially, the weaknesses and vulnerabilities
of radical mass movements. As a result, political prisoners
serve collective prison time for all those who participated in
the movements from which they emerged. And because, as
James Baldwin once wrote, "a people who trust their history
do not find themselves immobilized in it," activists and organizers have a responsibility to know where we come from.


## MILITANCY AND RAISING THE STAKES

The liberal international human rights community often
defines political internees as those incarcerated for their
beliefs, not necessarily their actions. While such instances
abound, they are not the only or even the best examples of
politically motivated incarceration. Whether someone "did
it" ought not to determine fully who receives our support.
Instead, political prisoners are best conceived as active participants in resistance movements.

Thus the central issue for thinking about political prisoners is not whether they "did it" but what movements did
they come from and what are the broader circumstances
surrounding their arrest. Most of those incarcerated participated in radical movements seeking fundamental overhauls
of structures of power. Some of these, most notably several
former members of the Black Panther Party, are victims of
state frame-ups. But many others were active participants
in liberation struggles that included involvement in illegal
activities. Regardless of which side of the law their actions
fell on, however, America's political prisoners participated
in movements presenting revolutionary Left challenges to
the capitalist state; for many, these politics emerged out of
an explicit commitment to fighting white supremacy, and,
for some, patriarchy. These politics necessitated direct, confrontational responses to the violence of U.S. imperialism

and corporate hegemony—from war overseas to murderous attacks on people of color in the United States, from environmental destruction to the stark repression of incarceration itself. Political prisoners emerged from movements seeking to stop, to overturn, to develop alternatives to state and extralegal violence of the system. All of America's political internees did something; some resisted with force, some put their bodies on the line, and others used words and propagated ideas the state deemed too powerful to let slide as just so much free speech. The issue of political prisoners is less one of "innocence" than of defending people's ability and capacity to resist.

Of those incarcerated for engaging in illegal, often clandestine actions, most followed a similar path: several years of legal activism led to a determined belief in the need to raise the stakes. Their backgrounds are varied; prior to being activists, they were good-hearted progressives or class-conscious workers, apolitical moderates, or "red diaper babies." They spent years protesting, petitioning, organizing, and engaging in civil disobedience. But, time after time, frustration at the limited possibilities of available (i.e., legal) remedies to such entrenched injustice led many activists to seek—and many more to support—alternative options of resistance. This search for alternatives emerged from a desperation, it is true, but also from a palpable belief in the possibility of a more successful revolutionary politics. Building a movement, many have argued, requires an infrastructure hidden from the eyes and ears of the state—especially as repression becomes more intense. Although it often meant a turn to armed struggle, the search for new mechanisms of engaging in political action did not necessarily lead to violence. What it did mean, across the board, was a belief in raising the stakes of resistance. Upping the ante through militant, often clandestine, tactics was not intended to stand in for organizing a mass movement (although sectarianism and different strategic priorities have often yielded this in effect if not in intent). Rather, militancy meant an ongoing commitment to develop a revolutionary movement that looked to create opportunities for expanded resistance in the context of concrete conditions.

There are several, somewhat overlapping communities of struggle from which America's political prisoners have emerged in recent decades. This book focuses on the most primary movements these prisoners have participated in: the Black and New Afrikan, Puerto Rican, Indigenous, and Chicano freedom struggles; antiracist solidarity and opposition to U.S. imperialism; revolutionary nonviolence against the state's ability to wage war; and, more recently, activists incarcerated for their actions on behalf of earth and animal liberation as well as information transparency and civil liberties. While my focus is on those facing the most severe sentences and tied to established political movements, readers should keep in mind that the United States has always had more political prisoners than can be summarized in one small book. Each wave of repression has not only targeted those who end up serving long sentences, but also many activists who go to jail rather than cooperate with grand jury investigations or who are targeted for their support of radical actions as well as those who maintain family and community ties despite incarceration. Many people have passed in and out of prison on a variety of politically motivated charges and not always based on longstanding connection to social movements. There are many examples, for instance, of women and trans people being incarcerated for fighting back against or killing their abusers. The 2007 convictions of four young Black lesbians in New York City for defending themselves from a homophobic attack, the imprisonment of Black transwoman CeCe McDonald since 2012 for similarly defending herself against physical abuse, and the twenty-year sentence Black mother Marissa Alexander received for firing a gun in the air to ward off her abusive husband are exceptional only for being somewhat well-known. The urgency of many acts of resistance makes hard and fast rules of defining political prisoners a risky endeavor. What follows, then, is an introductory and incomplete sketch of some of the revolutionary struggles that have produced America's political prisoners.

# North American Freedom Struggles

THE THREE DECADES FOLLOWING WORLD WAR II, ROUGHLY 1945 TO 1975, WITNESSED an array of upheavals around the world that continue to influence the political, economic, social, and cultural landscape. Perhaps the most important development internationally was the success of anticolonialism. With European colonial powers stretched thin by a costly world war, radical and revolutionary movements throughout the Third World of Africa, Asia, and Latin America began achieving independence or emerging triumphant against Western-supported dictators in their own countries. In most cases, these movements attempted to replace the corrupt regime with some form of socialism. Most of these Third World liberation movements struggled for independence from the colonial regimes or the overturning of neocolonial regimes that had controlled their countries for decades or generations. The list of victories was impressive and seemed permanently expanding: beginning with China in 1948, there were successful revolutions or triumphs by popular movements in Ghana (1957), Guinea (1958), Cuba (1959), Cameroon, Togo, Senegal and Mali (1960), Algeria (1962), Chile (1970), Guinea Bissau (1974), Angola and Mozambique (1975), Vietnam, Cambodia, and Laos (1975), Grenada (1979), Nicaragua and Iran (1979), Zimbabwe (1980), Namibia (1991), South Africa (1994), and dozens of others. Such sweeping and at least initially radical change defined the Third World as a political project in its own right, separate from either the capitalist First World or the bureaucratic communism of the Second World—although some national liberation movements did align with the Soviet Union or China and received much-needed material aid from the "socialist camp." These movements united revolutionary nationalism with some form of socialism and an eclectic range of tactics to achieve independence. While recent history has shown capitalism's ability to colonize without formal armies, as well as the problem of leftist authoritarian rule, the sweeping tide of revolution seemed to leave no country unaffected in the two-decade period known as "the Sixties."

About Time Black Panther Archives / Dan O'Neil

*Soledad Brothers George Jackson, Fleeta Drumgo, and John Clutchette in a police van, circa 1971.*

## BLACK LIBERATION AND SETTLER COLONIALISM

Within the United States, the Third World socialist project was most forcefully articulated by the Black liberation struggle. Through the internationalist politics of many leaders and rank-and-file activists, Black liberationists identified their cause with anticolonial resistance overseas. More than affinity, however, this unity was born of a similar designated status. As the Sixties wore on, many radicals began to speak of peoples of color in the United States as "internal colonies," captive nations within a "settler colonial" empire. Rather than a colonial government serving a faraway power, settler colonies are those countries—the United States, Israel, Canada, South Africa, Australia, New Zealand—established through the settlement of foreign populations as dominant classes and the imposition of institutions and structures upon a displaced and marginalized Indigenous population. Settler colonialism in the Americas is based on both the slaughter and containment of the Indigenous population, as well as the subjugation and control of African slaves and their descendants.

Viewing the situation of Black people and other peoples of color as one of internal colonialism was a natural complement to the militant politics already developing within the movement. This analysis joined race and class as constituent elements of colonial rule: the nations internal to the United States were the most oppressed populations, where race served as a marker of class distinction. The goal was to liberate the captive nations—and, as Black Liberation Army soldier Mtayari Shabaka Sundiata once put it, "How can we talk about a nation and not talk about an army?"

While the armed actions of the 1970s marked a different phase of the Black liberation movement, this shift was not as unprecedented as some have suggested. The civil rights movement was never as nonviolent as it has been traditionally depicted; sections of it were always armed (most famously the Deacons for Defense), and even the unarmed aspects were constantly seeking to raise the stakes of resistance to white supremacy. Groups like the Revolutionary Action Movement worked behind the scenes in the early to mid-1960s to develop both Black nationalist consciousness and the capacity for armed resistance. As civil rights activists became more effective and with the quick growth of a self-consciously Black Power movement, the struggle for Black liberation clashed with an entrenched white supremacist power structure and increasingly repressive state.

The Black Panther Party (BPP) was the best-known of the revolutionary nationalist formations in the late 1960s. Born in Oakland in 1966, the Panthers had grown to a nationwide organization in just two years. It was, as former New York Panther Jamal Joseph has said, a Black organization rooted in class struggle. Panther chapters in cities across the country built a series of community programs; the best-known entailed community defense, whereby Party members would observe police officers making arrests in an attempt to thwart brutality or stop the arrest altogether. The Panthers also engaged in free community healthcare and breakfast for children programs, among other "survival pending revolution" operations. With the full weight of state repression against them, the Panthers soon began racking up political prisoners on charges big and small. And the repression wasn't just based on imprisonment; part of the FBI's campaign against the Panthers, as codified in its Counterintelligence Program (COINTELPRO), entailed spreading distrust within the group and between the Panthers and other radical groups. Sometimes these FBI-fostered hostilities degenerated into violence; for instance, the shooting deaths of Panther activists John Huggins and Bunchy Carter in early 1969, ostensibly by members of a rival organization, were in fact provoked by the police. Police had already killed Bobby Hutton, one of the first to join the Panthers, on April 6, 1968, and a dozen other Panthers were felled by police by 1970. In addition to the murder of Panther activists, both leaders and rank-and-file activists found themselves facing a variety of charges for acts real and imagined.

Such repression bred a climate of fear and distrust internally, as well as a push toward clandestine armed struggle. Black communities had been increasingly in open revolt against the state, especially the police; there were hundreds of rebellions in cities across the country between 1964 and 1968 (dubbed "urban riots"). In that climate, several police officers were killed, and the government increasingly looked to blame Black Panther activists for any attack against police or, for that matter, white people in general. LA Black Panther Romaine "Chip" Fitzgerald, for instance, remains in prison from a 1969 shootout with police. This climate made it easy for the state to frame Black radicals. To name just a few cases: Panther leaders Dhoruba Bin-Wahad in New York and Geronimo ji-Jaga Pratt in California both served time in prison (nineteen and twenty-seven years, respectively) for attacks of which the state knew they were innocent. Mondo we Langa (formerly David Rice) and Ed Poindexter in Nebraska continue to serve time on trumped-up charges, as do Marshall Eddie Conway in Maryland and Herman Bell and Jalil Muntaqim of the New York 3. (Their codefendant, Albert "Nuh" Washington, died of cancer in prison in April 2000 after almost thirty years inside.)

Two instances of repression particularly stand out in the formation of a Black underground: in a predawn raid on December 4, 1969, Chicago police murdered Mark Clark and Fred Hampton, the twenty-one-year-old leader of that city's Panther chapter. Police fired almost a hundred bullets into the apartment, unprovoked, seriously wounding Hampton as he slept (a police informant had drugged him to ensure his slumber) and then finishing him off execution-style with two bullets to the head, fired at point-blank range. Four days later, Los Angeles police attempted a similar predawn raid on the Panther office there, though the chapter was prepared and survived the assault. The message was unmistakable: the government was bent on destroying the Black Panther Party by any means necessary.

The other key incident at this time was the April 1969 indictment of twenty-one Black Panthers from the BPP's New York chapter for a host of fabricated, violent conspiracies. Although all were acquitted by the jury in less than an hour, the trial lasted two years, during which time most of the accused remained in prison, as bail had been set at $100,000 each. Even without securing convictions, the government had managed to remove most of the leadership and key activists of the New York chapter. And during those two years, internal divisions within the Panthers had become unbridgeable, as BPP cofounder Huey Newton expelled many members of the New York 21, as they were collectively known, for questioning his leadership. Many of the defendants from that case either went into exile with the international chapter of the Panthers or they went underground to help form the Black Liberation Army (BLA).

The BLA emerged in a climate of heightened police repression, not only against Black liberation activists, but against the Black community at large. Police shootings and killings of unarmed civilians, including children, had become a regular feature of urban life by the late 1960s. Viewing the police as an occupying army, the BLA crafted a response of guerrilla warfare. While the idea, and perhaps even the infrastructure, for the BLA had long been in the making, the organization announced its presence through armed attacks against police as retaliation, not against individual officers but against police violence in general. In 1971 alone, the FBI claimed that the BLA carried out more than a dozen attacks on officers in California, Georgia, New Jersey, New York, and Pennsylvania. The BLA claimed responsibility for several of these in communiqués sent to the media. Between 1971 and 1981, at least eight alleged BLA members were killed in shootouts with police, and more than two dozen were arrested. In many cases, the shooting was initiated by police, and the alleged BLA members were then falsely accused of wounding or killing their attackers. Most notorious were the murder charges brought against Assata Shakur and Sundiata Acoli following their arrests on the New Jersey Turnpike in 1973 (in an incident where BLA member Zayd Shakur and a police officer were killed). Despite evidence showing their innocence, they were convicted in separate trials and sentenced to life. In addition to engaging the police in combat, the BLA also had a campaign against drug dealers in the ghettos, whom they saw as sapping the strength and vitality of Black communities; BLA prisoner Teddy Jah Heath, who died in prison in 2001, served twenty-eight years for the kidnapping of a drug dealer in which no one was hurt.

Lacking wealthy benefactors or steady access to resources, BLA cells often relied on bank robberies to secure funds (a tactic revolutionaries call "expropriations," for it involves taking money that capitalist institutions have secured through other people's labor and using it ostensibly to further liberatory ends). In a phenomenon other revolutionary groups would also experience, many BLA soldiers were captured engaging in these high-risk actions.

As members of a clandestine army fighting to free a colonized people, most captured BLA combatants have defined themselves as prisoners of war, not just political prisoners.

Several attempted to escape from prison, often with the help of units on the outside—sometimes successfully, at least for short periods of time. Among those still incarcerated for alleged BLA activities (and not mentioned above) are Russell "Maroon" Shoatz, Kojo Sababu, Joe-Joe Bowen, Bashir Hameed, and Abdul Majid. Meanwhile, after their release, former BLA soldiers and POW's, such as Ashanti Alston and Safiya Bukhari among many others, became stalwart organizers for the freedom of remaining prisoners.

By 1975, there was a lull in BLA activity, as many participants were on trial or in prison. At this time, the group's attention turned toward consolidating its political ideology through small-scale newsletters, a study manual, and communiqués. On the outside, however, others began rebuilding the BLA's capacity to carry out even grander actions than had been undertaken to date.

In November 1979, the BLA made an auspicious public reentry, helping Assata Shakur break out of prison in New Jersey; it was a daring escape, made more impressive by the fact that it succeeded with no injuries or fatalities. Shakur ultimately went into exile in Cuba, though the state continues to pursue her capture; in 2013, the FBI made Shakur the first woman on the "most wanted terrorist list" and the state of New Jersey offered $2 million bounty for her capture. Besides Shakur, ex-Panther Nehanda Abiodun remains in exile there, as does Puerto Rican independentista William Morales. News reports estimate that Cuba is home to ninety U.S. fugitives, although it is unclear how many of them fled political persecution, nor is Cuba the only place housing U.S. exiles. Former Panthers Pete and Charlotte O'Neal are exiled in Tanzania, and Don Cox lived in France for more than three decades until his 2011 death.

Units of the BLA continued. Two years after Shakur's escape, in October 1981, several people attempted to rob a Brink's armored car in Nyack, New York, about thirty miles north of New York City. The expropriation would have netted $1.6 million which, according to a communiqué issued two weeks later under the name Revolutionary Armed Task

Force of the BLA, was to have helped fund continued clandestine endeavors and other Black community programs. But the action went awry: a shootout at the Brink's truck left a security guard dead, and two police officers were killed at a roadblock in an exchange of gunfire a few miles away, as the radicals attempted to flee. Four militants were captured at the scene, including BLA member Sam Brown and three white allies—Kathy Boudin, David Gilbert, and Judy Clark. (Boudin and Gilbert were former members of the Weather Underground and had been living clandestinely for some time; Clark was a leader of the aboveground May 19th Communist Organization; the three were not at the scene of the robbery itself but were arrested at the police roadblock.) A shootout in Queens, New York, two days later left BLA soldier Mtayari Shabaka Sundiata dead and Sekou Odinga in police custody. Police tortured Odinga, burning him with cigarettes, removing his toenails, and rupturing his pancreas during long beatings that left him hospitalized for six months.

In the weeks that followed, an FBI dragnet created a climate of hysteria, sweeping up many other activists, some of whom had nothing to do with the Brink's incident (and several of whom were ultimately acquitted of all charges). All told, more than a dozen people were arrested leading to multiple trials, at both the state and federal levels, emanating from the Brink's robbery and the escape of Assata Shakur. Additionally, several aboveground supporters and friends, both Black and white, served time for refusing to testify before grand juries investigating these matters. While many from these assorted trials have since been released, several remain in prison with what,

The Jericho Movement

*Sekou Odinga*

for most of them, amount to life sentences. Clark, Gilbert, and BLA member Kuwasi Balagoon—a veteran of the NY 21 case—were convicted on state felony murder charges in 1983 and sentenced to seventy-five years to life. In another state trial, BLA member Sekou Odinga was convicted of attempted murder and sentenced to twenty-five years to life for returning fire against the cops shooting at him prior to his arrest.

In a move that would be repeated in later cases brought against left-wing radicals, federal prosecutors in the Brink's case used the RICO (Racketeer Influenced and Corrupt Organizations) Act, originally intended for prosecuting the Mafia, to try those they claimed were involved in illegal underground activity. (RICO allows guilt-by-association "conspiracies" to be prosecuted as criminal enterprises). In the 1983 federal trial, Odinga and white anti-imperialist Silvia Baraldini (another May 19th Communist Organization leader) were found guilty of racketeering and conspiracy in connection with an attempted bank expropriation and Assata Shakur's escape, each receiving a forty-year sentence. Three codefendants facing robbery-murder charges, former Panthers Chui Ferguson and Jamal Joseph and Republic of New Afrika activist Bilal Sunni-Ali, were acquitted of the RICO charges, although Ferguson and Joseph were convicted of accessory charges and received twelve-year sentences. Balagoon and Odinga had attempted to be tried together to collectively mount a POW defense, but they were tried separately (Balagoon by New York State, Odinga by the federal government). Still, both invoked international law in claiming the right to resist unjust rule by force.

Balagoon died of AIDS in prison on December 13, 1986, and Odinga remains incarcerated. Brown was convicted in 1984. (Brown and Clark are not considered political prisoners: Brown was tortured after his arrest and denied medical care until he cooperated with authorities, yet he still received a life sentence, which he serves under protective custody for being a government witness. In the late 1980s, Clark asked to be removed from political prisoner lists.) Kathy Boudin, who pleaded guilty in 1984 to felony murder and robbery, was sentenced to twenty years to life; she was granted parole and released from prison in 2003. Marilyn Buck and Mutulu Shakur were convicted of racketeering and conspiracy in a federal trial in 1988; Buck received fifty years (on top of twenty years for an earlier conviction), Shakur sixty years.

A later case that the FBI falsely dubbed "Son of Brink's" and a "successor" to the BLA involved an attack on another group of Black revolutionary nationalists: In October 1984, eight members of the aboveground Sunrise Collective— Lateefah Carter, Coltrane Chimurenga, Omowale Clay, Yvette Kelley, Colette Pean, Viola Plummer, Robert Taylor, and Roger Wareham—were arrested in a set of massive, military-style police raids around New York City. They were charged with conspiracy to rob banks and break out Balagoon and Odinga from prison. Using a new "preventive detention" law pushed through Congress by then-President Reagan supposedly to combat the Mafia, prosecutors led by U.S. attorney Rudolph Giuliani convinced a judge to deny bail to the activists—none of whom had any criminal record—as "dangers to the community" and they were all held for several months. The case became known as the New York Eight+ (a ninth, Latino activist José Ríos, was charged later), and it sparked major headlines, mass organizing, and a packed trial. Despite extensive video and audio surveillance and testimony by an informant in the group, in August 1985 the jury acquitted all defendants of the major charges. They were convicted only of minor charges—seven of possession of illegal weapons and one of possession of false IDs; Ríos was acquitted on all counts. In interviews afterward, jurors condemned the FBI surveillance and the prosecutors' "guilt by association" tactics. One defendant (Pean) received three months' jail time; the others got probation and community service. (These activists later became the core of the December 12th Movement, which has done much work internationally and at the United Nations to highlight the human rights violations against Black political prisoners and the demand for reparations for Black people.) The New York Eight+ case also led to an investigative grand jury that subpoenaed many

Black community members and jailed several who refused to cooperate for months.

Several of those tried for alleged involvement in the second generation of the BLA—including the Assata escape and Brink's debacle, but also several other robberies and attacks during the late 1970s—were citizens of the Provisional Government of the Republic of New Afrika (PG-RNA), a Black nationalist group formed in 1968. The PG-RNA took the internal colonialism thesis a step further. They proclaimed Alabama, Georgia, Louisiana, Mississippi, and South Carolina—the five states of the Black Belt South, where slavery was most concentrated—as the territory of the Black Nation. (The RNA's position here revived and revised one held by the Communist Party in the 1930s.) The RNA developed the governmental apparatus of the Black Nation and organized for independence, choosing Mississippi as its base. Following Brink's, the Joint Terrorism Task Force (a collaborative effort of various police agencies and the FBI) raided RNA territory in Mississippi to arrest several activists. Some were brought to a federal trial emanating from Brink's; others refused to cooperate with grand jury investigations. These arrests were not the first time RNA activists found themselves behind bars. Most famously, eleven RNA citizens were arrested in 1971 in the first military assault on the group's headquarters, which coincided with arrests at a residence where several members lived. While the government had a warrant to arrest one person (who, it turned out, was not there), police officials fired three hundred rounds into the PG-RNA government office. PG-RNA officials returned fire, and in the melee a police officer was killed. All eleven were charged with his death, even though four of the eleven were arrested later and at a different location. Two RNA activists also served five years for gun possession at the 1972 Democratic National Convention in Miami; authorities speciously claimed the pair was there to assassinate the Democratic nominee.

At the same time as Black Power was blossoming in the "free world," its revolutionary potential energized thousands behind prison walls, most of whom had not been previously active and were not incarcerated for consciously political offenses. The most famous example in the 1970s was George Jackson; arrested for participating in a petty robbery as a teenager, Jackson was given the brutally vague sentence of one year to life. Jackson discovered politics while in prison, studying voraciously and ultimately becoming a field marshal of the Black Panther Party. His 1970 book *Soledad Brother* became a bestseller, and Jackson became a symbol and strategist of revolutionary opposition. His second book, the posthumously published *Blood in My Eye*, was viewed as a manual for Black guerrilla activity. Jackson, John Clutchette, and Fleeta Drumgo were charged in January 1970 with killing a corrections officer in retaliation for guards having shot and killed three prisoners in the yard. Defense committees for the "Soledad Brothers," as they were known, sprouted up across the country, bringing together nationalists, communists, and assorted radicals.

On August 7, 1970, Jackson's seventeen-year-old brother, Jonathan, attempted a daring raid at Marin County Courthouse. Although George was not in court that day, Jonathan gave guns to three prisoners who were there participating in a trial: William Christmas, James McClain, and Ruchell Magee. The group took the judge, prosecutor, and several jurors hostage, demanding the state free George and other political prisoners. As they attempted to escape in a van, guards on hand from nearby San Quentin prison—where Christmas, McClain, and Magee were incarcerated—opened fire, killing Jackson, Christmas, McClain, and the judge, and seriously wounding Magee and the prosecutor. Magee was acquitted on the most serious charges against him but convicted of kidnapping and sentenced, again, to a life sentence. Incarcerated since 1963, Magee remains in prison in 2013.

Angela Davis, a Black member of the Communist Party and the Soledad Brothers Defense Committee who was close with George Jackson, was charged with kidnapping and murder following Jonathan's raid, after it was discovered that some of the guns used were licensed in her name. (The younger Jackson had been serving as Davis's bodyguard at the time.) Davis wrote about the plight and politics of prisoners during her incarceration. Davis went underground in the post-raid hysteria but was arrested two months later. She spent sixteen months in pretrial detention, much of it in solitary. After a worldwide campaign demanding her freedom, she was acquitted in 1972 and has continued to participate in the anti-prison movement and write and lecture about the prison system.

George Jackson, however, was killed in San Quentin. In the span of thirty minutes on August 21, 1971, Jackson led prisoners in the seizure of the isolation unit where he and twenty-six other prisoners were being held. During the revolt, two white prisoners and three guards were killed. Guards then shot and killed Jackson in the prison yard. Prison officials claimed that Jackson was trying to escape, though oddities in the state's case and the ample evidence that law enforcement wanted to kill Jackson cast doubt over the official explanation. In fact, both sides might be correct: Jackson could have been planning an escape, and the state could have set him up to be killed. After the incident, one of Jackson's lawyers and six of the most outspoken prisoners were charged with conspiracy and murder for the five deaths other than Jackson's that occurred that day. The attorney, Steve Bingham, and three of the prisoners—Fleeta Drumgo, Luis Talamantez, and Willie Sundiata Tate—were acquitted. One prisoner, David Johnson, was convicted of assault and freed shortly thereafter. One prisoner, Johnny Spain, was convicted of conspiracy and two counts of murder but later freed on a technicality. Hugo Pinell, who had also become a revolutionary while in prison, was convicted of assault and sentenced to life in prison. He remains incarcerated. Pinell has since been subject to one of the longest periods of strict isolation of any prisoner in the world; he has spent more than forty years in solitary confinement, the last twenty-four of which have been at California's notorious Pelican Bay Security Housing Unit. He last appeared before the parole board in 2008, at which time his release was once again denied and he was given a further fifteen years before his next hearing.

Jackson's death helped spark one of the most famous prison rebellions in this period. Prisoners at Attica Correctional Facility in western New York State held a silent protest and fast to honor Jackson. This demonstration followed steady organizing that prisoners had been doing to improve their conditions, and the show of solidarity among the prisoners frightened the authorities. The increasing tension boiled over weeks later, when prisoners seized control of the prison in what started as an inchoate riot but quickly turned into a highly political rebellion. Prisoners maintained control of Attica for four days, holding negotiations with the state to not only end the standoff but improve conditions in the prison and advance a revolutionary response to state power. It ended brutally, however, when Governor Nelson Rockefeller ordered troops to retake the prison, leaving forty-three people dead (police killed ten guards who had been held as hostages and twenty-nine prisoners; insurgents killed one police officer during the initial scuffle that led to the riot, as well as four other prisoners during the rebellion).

The Attica rebellion reflected a growing radicalism among prisoners that had yielded increased pressure, both inside and out, on the prison system as a whole. The late 1960s and early 1970s witnessed a rising prison movement, including dozens of riots, work strikes, escape attempts, and the formation of prisoner labor unions. Following Jackson's example, Herman Wallace, Robert Wilkerson, and Albert Woodfox formed a prison chapter of the Black Panther Party in Louisiana's notoriously brutal Angola prison, which is a former plantation. The trio had a history of involvement with the Panthers, though they were serving time on separate robbery charges. To stop their organizing, prison officials charged them with murder, won convictions based on concocted evidence, and placed them in solitary confinement. Wilkerson was released in 2001, having been found innocent on appeal of the charges for which he had served almost thirty years. Meanwhile, after thirty-six years of isolation, legal appeals, and an international pressure campaign succeeded in removing Wallace and Woodfox from solitary confinement in March 2008. In July 2008 and February 2013, Woodfox's conviction has been overturned three times, most recently by a federal judge in February 2013, but the state appeals. He and Wallace remain incarcerated in isolation as of September 2013. That summer, Wallace was diagnosed with terminal liver cancer and given months to live. He was freed by a judge's order on October 1, 2013, and died three days later.

In the decades since George Jackson, the Attica Rebellion, and the conviction of the Angola 3, New Afrikan politics have continued to permeate America's prisons—at least among men—with numerous Black men declaring themselves conscious citizens of New Afrika committed and becoming outspoken proponents of various forms of revolutionary Black and New Afrikan nationalism. (Khalfani Khaldun, Shaka N'Zinga, Kevin "Rashid" Johnson and Sanyika Shakur are a few of the better-known examples). These men were politicized in the age of mass incarceration: their political activity took place amid the hyperpolicing and brutal conditions of confinement that have characterized working-class Black

*An example of Kevin "Rashid" Johnson's artwork, calling attention to the existence of political prisoners across the United States. For more see rashidmod.com*

life since the early 1970s. George Jackson is something of a founding father for this political trajectory and remains an inspiration to many. It is no accident that, forty years after his death in San Quentin, mere possession of one of George Jackson's books is enough to get a California prisoner sent into one of the state's long-term isolation units. Whether such people—not active before incarceration, but now targeted for repression inside the prisons because of their political opinions or simply their reading habits—are "political prisoners" is a point of some debate. Yet their contributions to contemporary prison struggles are clear.

These politicized prisoners show that the roots of Black political prisoners are more varied roots than just the politics of national liberation. The Philadelphia-based MOVE organization is another case in point. MOVE organization began in the 1970s around the philosophy of a working-class Black man named John Africa. Members of the group chose the last name Africa and lived collectively, ate vegan, and staged militant protests against both police violence and animal abuse. The notoriously racist Philadelphia police, under the leadership of police commissioner turned-mayor Frank Rizzo, developed an instant hatred of MOVE. Through public protest and a loudspeaker attached to their communal West Philadelphia home, MOVE members mocked police authority (while also antagonizing some of their neighbors). The police, meanwhile, routinely attacked MOVE demonstrations. The situation first came to a head in 1978, when police attempted to enforce a court order mandating MOVE to vacate its house. MOVE refused the order, and by August, police had laid siege to the house in an effort to drive a resource-strapped MOVE out. On August 8, the efforts to remove MOVE erupted in violence: six hundred police officers used guns and fire hoses to drive the activists from the basement where they were hiding. Officer James Ramp was shot and killed in the melee. Although Ramp was standing in front of the house and was shot from behind and even though MOVE members were in the basement of the house, the nine adults inside were arrested, but not before three officers beat

Delbert Africa on camera as he surrendered to them, clearly unarmed. Police officers bulldozed the house and destroyed any evidence that might exculpate MOVE members, who were tried and collectively sentenced to thirty to one hundred years for Ramp's death. Merle Africa died of cancer in prison in 1998, and seven of the other eight MOVE prisoners were denied parole in spring 2008, as was Chuck Africa when he came up for parole in October of that year. They remain in prison as of 2013. As is typical in cases involving high-profile prisoners, both those incarcerated for their political activism and those who become politicized inside, part of the reason the MOVE members were supposedly denied parole is the "severity of their crime"—which never changes and thus becomes a convenient excuse for indefinitely prolonging incarceration.

Standoffs between police and MOVE continued; tensions spilled over again in 1985, when another siege of the new MOVE home culminated in city police dropping an FBI-supplied bomb on the house, killing eleven people, including MOVE founder John Africa and five children, and destroying much of the block. Even before the bombing, however, successive mayoral administrations from Frank Rizzo to Wilson Goode virulently chastised anyone, including reporters, who challenged their authority or decision to act violently against MOVE. A radio journalist named Mumia Abu-Jamal, a former leader of the city's Panther chapter and sympathetic to MOVE, particularly attracted the city's ire with his frequent reports highlighting police brutality and corruption. Late at night on December 9, 1981, while driving a taxi to

Joe Piette / Workers World

supplement his income, Abu-Jamal saw his brother being beaten by police officer Daniel Faulkner. He stepped out of his cab to intervene, at which point both he and Faulkner were shot. Although several witnesses claim they saw others flee the scene, Abu-Jamal was the only person seriously considered as a suspect and was quickly charged with Faulkner's murder. At trial, Judge Albert Sabo denied Abu-Jamal the right to have an attorney of his choosing (MOVE founder John Africa) and also denied Abu-Jamal the right to defend himself, even removing him from the courtroom during most of the proceedings. A witness heard Judge Sabo, notoriously eager to send people to the electric chair, utter a racial slur and a commitment to "fry" Abu-Jamal. The prosecutor, in a practice later found unconstitutional by the U.S. Supreme Court in another case, used Abu-Jamal's past political affiliation with the Black Panthers as an argument to the jury for the death penalty. In July 1982, Abu-Jamal was sentenced to death; since the 1990s, he has been the country's best-known political prisoner.

Mumia's international support movement has succeeded in preventing his execution and has even extracted momentary legal openings. Each level of appeal has, however, quickly closed those openings by reaffirming Mumia's conviction, despite significant evidence of prosecutorial, police, and judicial misconduct, and adamantly denied him the new and fair trial that Amnesty International and many other legal organizations have demanded. In 2001, U.S. District Court Judge William Yohn affirmed Mumia's conviction but voided his death sentence, citing "irregularities" in the original sentencing. The judge converted the sentence to life without parole and gave the prosecution the option to conduct a new sentencing hearing in accordance with legal procedures to determine whether Mumia would be sentenced to death. Both sides appealed. In March 2008, the U.S. Third Circuit Court of Appeals again upheld Mumia's conviction and in July 2008 the full Third Circuit rejected his request to rehear the appeal. But there still remains the possibility of a new trial if the Supreme Court accepts the case and if it overturns the conviction. The Appeals Court also affirmed the lower court's voiding of Mumia's death sentence. After a period in solitary confinement, Mumia was transferred to general population in 2012. He continues to fight his conviction and his new sentence of life in prison.

Warren K. Leffler
Library of Congress LC-DIG-ds-00753

## THE AMERICAN INDIAN MOVEMENT

The American Indian Movement (AIM) formed in Minnesota in 1968 and was always strongest in the western half of the country. Founded by four Indigenous activists, two of whom were formerly incarcerated, AIM set out to apply the militant community organizing model of the Black Panthers to Indigenous communities and conditions in cities and reservations. One of its first actions was to support the nineteen-month occupation of Alcatraz, the abandoned island prison off the coast of San Francisco, that an ad hoc group of Indigenous activists had seized. The proclamation announcing the occupation declared that reservations already resembled abandoned prisons. The group also launched daring marches, such as the Trail of Broken Treaties, a national caravan that ended in Washington, DC, in 1972 with a twenty-point plan to improve the status of Indigenous people in the United States. A similar march in 1978, the Longest Walk, stretched from Alcatraz to the capital.

By the early 1970s, as the Panthers declined, in part due to state violence, AIM had become the FBI's new number-one enemy. Dozens of AIM activists were murdered, some openly by police or vigilantes employed by corrupt tribal leaders, and the group was disrupted through a web of informants and misinformation. Most of the leadership—Dennis Banks, Vernon and Clyde Bellecourt, Leonard Crow Dog, Russell Means, John Trudell, and others—found themselves in and out of jail for participating in civil disobedience actions or simply for being outspoken in their opposition to U.S. colonialism. Their houses were routinely raided, and police openly surveilled their activities.

Besides the FBI, a state-sanctioned paramilitary outfit known as the Guardians of the Oglala Nation (GOONs) became the vanguard counterinsurgency force. Head GOON Dick Wilson called for an all-out war against AIM, and he did his part to deliver it, using the GOONs as an unofficial death squad in the Pine Ridge area. The repression was stark. People affiliated with the GOONs were suspected of murdering several AIM activists and supporters, presumably with the collusion of police and other law enforcement officials. For instance, on October 17, 1973, leader of the Independent Oglala Nation, Pedro Bissonnette was murdered by a GOON at a Bureau of Indian Affairs roadblock. GOON violence created a climate of terror throughout Pine Ridge, together with ubiquitous police and FBI harassment. Several AIM activists and supporters were killed throughout the 1970s. In one of the most gruesome incidents, longtime AIM activist Tina Trudell, her mother, and her three children were burned to death in an arson attack on their Nevada home on February 11, 1979. The attack occurred twelve hours after her husband, fellow AIM activist John Trudell, burned an upside-down American flag outside FBI headquarters during a rally in support of Leonard Peltier. There was no official investigation into the attack. A fiery spokesman for AIM, Trudell and his family had long been targets of state harassment.

In 1973, AIM occupied the hamlet of Wounded Knee, the site of an infamous massacre of Indigenous people in 1890.

The occupation lasted from February to May, during which time AIM operated an autonomous territory despite being surrounded by several federal law enforcement agencies and GOON vigilantes. The action generated solidarity from activists across the country seeking to assist AIM by breaking through the police blockade meant to deprive the occupation of any food or other resources; in one of the most auspicious attempts, a group of activists (including several from Vietnam Veterans Against the War) chartered a plane to airdrop supplies. During the seventy-one-day occupation, there was constant gunfire exchanged between the state and AIM, leaving two AIM members dead. GOONs also "disappeared" twelve community members during this time. By May, AIM negotiated with the government to end the occupation. But it was hardly over.

Twelve hundred people were arrested in the immediate aftermath of Wounded Knee, and five hundred more were arrested over the next two years. Between 1973 and 1975, federal officials and GOONs engaged in an immense crackdown on Red Power. In the immediate aftermath of the occupation, the government charged seven activists with conspiracy. Much of AIM's top leadership was indicted. Two of them, Dennis Banks and Russell Means, had their case separated from the others (Clyde Bellecourt, Carter Camp, Leonard Crow Dog, Stan Holder, and Pedro Bissonnette). Both men were acquitted in 1974. The depths of FBI malice against the Wounded Knee occupation were so prevalent that seven jurors involved in the trial publicly petitioned for any remaining cases to be dismissed. Several judges in other cases did dismiss most of the other cases, and most of those who went to trial were acquitted. In the other conspiracy case, Camp, Crow Dog, and Holder were convicted on reduced charges in 1975 and served brief jail terms. The case against Bellecourt was dismissed for lack of evidence, and Bissonnette was murdered before he could stand trial.

The repression continued. In June 1975, two FBI agents, driving in separate and unmarked cars, entered Pine Ridge reservation in search of a man wanted for questioning. The agents were fired upon; they radioed for backup but also returned fire. Both agents and an Indian man were killed in the exchange. Four months later, police arrested two AIM activists, Dino Butler and Bob Robideau, for the murders. A grand jury refused to indict Butler and Robideau on grounds of self-defense.

A third man, Leonard Peltier, was also suspected in the defensive effort: Peltier had served as bodyguard for AIM cofounder Dennis Banks, participating in the group's Trail of Broken Treaties in 1972 and moving to the Pine Ridge reservation in 1973 to help in the defense of Wounded Knee. He was found in Canada, where he had fled in fear of reprisals stemming from the firefight, and was extradited to the United States and tried a year later. The government changed its strategy to ensure a conviction of Peltier. The new approach included a change of venue to a town known for its prejudice against Native people, a conservative judge, and ample new evidence—much of it perjured or otherwise questionable. The FBI also assigned agents to "protect" the judge and jury; similar actions were used later in one of the Brink's trials to the same effect. While there had been no threats against jurors and never an instance where radicals had tampered

with trials, the state used such tactics to instill fear among the very people who have to sit in judgment against the accused. As a result, Peltier received two consecutive life sentences, and has since become one of the best-known and longest-held political prisoners in the world.

Peltier's time in prison has not been without incident. Standing Deer, an Indigenous prisoner at Marion (a control-unit prison in Illinois), exposed a government plot to kill Peltier in 1978 and worked to protect Peltier's safety. Six years later, the pair entered a forty-two-day fast to win protections for Native spiritual practice in prison. The hunger strike received international attention and won some concessions, though it also resulted in both men being placed in solitary confinement for fifteen months with nothing but a bed and a toilet. His principled commitments throughout his time in prison earned Standing Deer much respect and admiration as a politically conscious and active prisoner. Standing Deer was released on September 4, 2001, after twenty-five years in prison, and immediately jumped into organizing to free Peltier and other political prisoners. He was murdered in his apartment on January 20, 2003, by a houseguest with whom he had argued.

Not all Indigenous political prisoners have been affiliated with AIM. Eddie Hatcher, a community activist in Robeson County, North Carolina, took over the offices of a local newspaper in 1988 to protest corruption in the area. Specifically, Hatcher and his comrade, Timothy Jacobs, took twenty journalists hostage to protest rampant police murder, the local government's involvement in drug trafficking, and the silence surrounding these issues. The men released their hostages unharmed when the governor agreed to their demand to establish an independent investigation of their allegations. Hatcher was acquitted by a jury for the action, but was indicted a second time, on federal kidnapping charges. After a brief stint underground, he was captured and sentenced to eighteen years in prison. He was given early parole in 1995, however, after being stabbed four times with an icepick and contracting HIV in prison. He was arrested again, this time for murder of a local resident, a charge for which he maintains his innocence. He was convicted and sentenced to life in prison in early 2001. He died in prison in May 2009.

Elspeth Meyer

## PUERTO RICAN INDEPENDENCE

Through centuries of Spanish colonialism, Puerto Rico generated a vibrant and militant independence movement that nearly drove out the Spanish before the U.S. invasion and occupation of 1898. With the arrival of a new colonizer, the resistance continued, providing as deep an opposition as any that U.S. settler colonialism has yet faced. There have been successive generations of struggle over the century since then. As under the Spanish, pro-independence activism has been continually and often brutally repressed. Throughout the 1930s and in the early 1950s, there were several uprisings against U.S. colonial rule. The Puerto Rican Nationalist Party—led by its president, Don Pedro Albizu Campos—played a fundamental role in organizing this resistance, which was met by police violence (for instance, a 1937 massacre in the town of Ponce killed nineteen and wounded two hundred), jailings, and blacklistings. Albizu was one of many

Nationalists who did long stints as political prisoners on U.S. soil; he died of cancer in 1964 after deliberate radiation poisoning in prison by U.S. authorities.

On October 30, 1950, after an island-wide uprising headquartered in the town of Jayuya, the colonial government declared martial law throughout Puerto Rico, and the United States brought in Air Force planes to bomb the temporarily liberated towns. Many activists were killed and hundreds were jailed. In response, seeking to bring world attention to this repression, U.S.-based Nationalist Party activists Oscar Collazo and Griselio Torresola attempted two days later to assassinate President Harry Truman. One of Truman's bodyguards was shot and killed, several others were wounded, Torresola was killed, and Collazo wounded, arrested, and ultimately sentenced to death. In response to an international campaign that gathered one hundred thousand signatures on Collazo's behalf, Truman later commuted the sentence to life in prison.

In March 1954, four other U.S.-based Nationalist Party activists, seeking to draw attention to the U.S. colonial control of the island, unfurled a Puerto Rican flag inside the U.S. House gallery of Congress and opened fire, wounding five Congressmen. Led by Lolita Lebrón, the action also involved Rafael Cancel Miranda, Irvin Flores, and Andrés Figueroa Cordero. It was timed to coincide with the Inter-American Conference in Caracas, Venezuela. The four were arrested and sentenced to life in prison. With a climate of terror and reprisals against independentistas both on the island and in the United States, the five Nationalists received limited open support throughout the 1950s and early 1960s.

The successful revolution in Cuba in 1959 helped create a rising tide of militancy within Puerto Rico, which snowballed throughout the 1960s as it made its way throughout the United States. Migration had created large communities of Puerto Ricans living in the United States who, influenced by the civil rights movement and developments within Puerto Rico and in the wider Third World, grew more radical as the decade wore on. The end of the decade witnessed a visible spike in Puerto Rican radicalism, which particularly took the form of antiwar, especially antidraft, resistance, and the upsurge in the pro-independence movement.

The Puerto Rican Left was a vibrant force throughout the 1960s and 1970s. Among the active organizations were, on the island, the Liga Socialista Puertorriqueña (LSP; Puerto Rican Socialist League) and the Partido Socialista Puertorriqueña (PSP; Puerto Rican Socialist Party), which also had a U.S. presence, and, in the United States, El Comité and, later, the Movimiento de Liberación Nacional (MLN; Movement for National Liberation). Inspired by the example of the Black Panthers, the Young Lords Party, initially a Chicago street gang turned political, initiated a host of community programs in the barrios of New York and Chicago. The organization combined a militant politics of community self-defense and a strong position against male chauvinism and for women's liberation with radical service (helping Spanish Harlem get garbage service and proper health care, for instance) and a diasporic strategy that connected Puerto Ricans in the United States to those on the island.

Armed struggle featured prominently in the Puerto Rican militancy of the 1960s and 1970s, both in the States and on the island. Juan Antonio Corretjer was an influential strategist of the independence movement, a former leader of both the Nationalist Party and the Puerto Rican Communist Party as well as a former political prisoner and one of the island's best-known poets; his influence is manifest throughout the Puerto Rican Left at this time, both aboveground and under. As secretary-general of the LSP, Corretjer outlined a strategy of people's war to build an independent and socialist Puerto Rico, situating this as part of the long tradition of Puerto Rican radicalism and within the context of the anticolonial revolutions then sweeping the globe, a way of unraveling the United States from within as well as from without.

As early as 1964, clandestine groups emerged in Puerto Rico, followed several years later by similar formations in the United States. These included the Comandos Armados de Liberación (CAL, Armed Commandos of Liberation),

Movimiento Independentista Revolucionario Armado (MIRA, Armed Revolutionary Independence Movement), and then, starting in the mid-1970s, the Comandos Revolucionarios del Pueblo (CRP, People's Revolutionary Commandos), the Fuerzas Armadas de Resistencia Popular (the Armed Forces of Popular Resistance), and the Organización de Voluntarios por la Revolución Puertorriqueña (OVRP, Organization of Volunteers for the Puerto Rican Revolution). The two most active, however, were the Fuerzas Armadas de Liberación Nacional (FALN; Armed Forces of National Liberation) and the Ejercito Popular Boricua (Puerto Rican Popular Army), also known as Los Macheteros, the Machete-Wielders. All of these underground organizations targeted U.S. military installations, police stations, federal agencies, U.S. banks, and department stores, among other sites selected for their role in helping uphold U.S. colonialism. In some cases they mounted joint actions.

The Macheteros were active almost exclusively in Puerto Rico; the FALN, in the United States. Between 1974 and 1983, by which time more than a dozen alleged members of the group had been arrested, the FALN claimed responsibility for more than 120 bombings against U.S. corporate or military targets. These attacks targeted property in all but one case: In January 1975, the FALN detonated a bomb during lunch hour at Fraunces Tavern, a New York City restaurant popular with Wall Street executives. The bomb killed four and wounded fifty people. (No one was ever charged with this bombing.) The accompanying communiqué claimed the bombing as a response to a restaurant bombing in Puerto Rico by CIA-connected right-wing Cubans that killed two independentistas and maimed ten other people—just the most recent in a wave of anti-independence terrorist attacks. Indeed, there would later be other U.S.-directed death-squad actions. Most notoriously, in July 1978, Puerto Rican police lured two young independentistas, whom they had recruited into a government-created underground group, to the top of a mountain called Cerro Maravilla, where they were executed in cold blood. After years of independentista campaigning

that forced Watergate-style hearings by the colonial legis-
lature (after the U.S. Justice Department refused to act), in
1984, ten police officers, including the head of the Intelligence
Division, were indicted, tried, convicted of various charges
related to the killings and their cover-up, and sentenced to
prison time. Two years later, the undercover agent who lured
the young men to their deaths—and who was never prosecuted—was assassinated in an action claimed by the clandestine OVRP.

In the 1970s, the campaign to end the lengthy incarceration of the five Puerto Rican Nationalists went into high gear:
The independence movement and its allies in the United
States and the Non-Aligned Movement of Third World
nations and liberation movements mounted an international
campaign for their release. In 1974, a diverse group of independence activists and their North American supporters, led
by the Puerto Rican Socialist Party, held a rally at Madison
Square Garden with twenty thousand people that identified Puerto Rican independence and the freeing of the five
Nationalists as central to a progressive agenda for the U.S.
Left. In one of the most attention-grabbing actions done as
part of the campaign, more than two dozen activists seized the
Statue of Liberty and hung a Puerto Rican flag on its crown
on October 30, 1977 (the anniversary of the thwarted 1950
uprising), using the media coverage to draw attention to the
ongoing incarceration of the Nationalists. Finally, in 1979,
feeling the pressure of this international campaign, President
Jimmy Carter granted unconditional release to Collazo,
Lebrón, Cancel Miranda, and Flores. (Carter had released
Andrés Figueroa Cordero in 1977; he was suffering from
cancer and passed away eighteen months after his release.)
They returned to Puerto Rico triumphant, though the ordeal
of Puerto Rican political incarceration was far from over.

By the time of the four Nationalists' freedom, the first
of what was soon to prove a new wave of arrests of Puerto
Rican independence fighters had occurred. In July 1978,
William Morales was arrested at the site of a bomb explosion
in Queens, New York, in which he lost part of both hands

Elspeth Meyer

THEY ARE SISTERS AND BROTHERS, WIVES AND HUSBANDS AND SONS AND DAUGHTERS AND FRIENDS WHO TAKE UP ARMS AGAINST THE OPPRESSOR.

and sight in one eye. While in custody, Morales was tortured by FBI agents. A longtime activist for Puerto Rican independence and socialism, he was accused of membership in the FALN and indicted on federal and state charges of possession of illegal weapons. Morales became the first of a new generation of imprisoned independentistas to refuse to participate in their own trials, asserting the position of prisoner of war, thus not subject to the colonial courts of the United States. Judges rejected that claim, and Morales was convicted and sentenced to a total of ninety-nine years. After a successful community pressure campaign to transfer him to a prison hospital for treatment of his eye and fitting his hands for prosthetic devices, Morales escaped, in an audacious action claimed by the FALN. In 1983, Interpol agents rearrested him in Mexico, and he served five years in prison there until a successful international campaign by the Puerto Rican independence movement and its Mexican and North American allies forced the Mexican government to defy the United States, which was seeking his extradition, and instead to fly him to Cuba, where he received political asylum and has been living ever since.

On April 4, 1980, eleven people suspected of involvement with the FALN were arrested outside Chicago. At least four others would be arrested over the next three years to also stand trial for alleged FALN involvement. As was standard in these cases of Puerto Rican revolutionaries, the accused refused to participate in their own trials, asserting their position as prisoners of war not subject to the colonial courts of the United States. The courts rejected these claims without a hearing and proceeded to try the defendants against their wishes and, therefore, often in their absence. Most were convicted of "seditious conspiracy"—organizing to overthrow the government—and given lengthy sentences amounting to life in prison. The youngest of the group, Luis Rosa, received the longest sentence—108 years—for federal and state charges, along with a contempt sentence. None of the alleged FALN members was convicted of harming or killing anyone.

Throughout the 1980s, other Puerto Rican independence groups continued to target U.S. colonialism. In 1981, the Macheteros blew up eleven U.S. military planes in Puerto Rico that were destined for use in El Salvador. But it was a daring bank expropriation for which they received the most attention. It occurred in Hartford, Connecticut, in 1983, when members of the group, including a bank employee, took $7.2 million from Wells Fargo without injury or arrest. On August 30, 1985, in a massive military operation that activists dubbed "the second invasion of Puerto Rico," thirteen independentistas were swept up, charged with planning or participating in the robbery, the biggest in U.S. history. Ultimately, nineteen people faced charges. They went through a series of trials in various groups; outcomes varied, including some convictions, some acquittals, some negotiated agreements, and some charges dismissed due to government misconduct. Several of these activists spent years in prison, the longest terms of which were served by Antonio Camacho Negrón (fifteen years) and Juan Segarra Palmer (nineteen years).

As with the earlier efforts to free the five Nationalists and William Morales, a lengthy and far-ranging international campaign finally proved successful in winning release of many of the remaining Puerto Rican political prisoners. In September 1999, President Bill Clinton offered clemency to more than a dozen, including fourteen people still incarcerated after fourteen to nineteen years and several Macheteros activists who still had fines pending. Twelve of those still in prison accepted the terms, under which eleven (Edwin Cortés, Elizam Escobar, Ricardo Jiménez, Adolfo Matos, Dylcia Pagán, Alberto Rodríguez, Alicia Rodríguez, Lucy Rodríguez, Luis Rosa, Alejandrina Torres, and Carmen Valentín) were immediately released and another (Segarra Palmer) had to serve five more years before being freed. Camacho Negrón was not offered a shortened term; he was released in 2004. Two people were not included in the original clemency offer but have since been freed: Carlos Alberto Torres was paroled in 2010; Haydée Beltrán Torres, who chose not to apply for clemency in the 1990s, was freed in 2009. One of the alleged FALN members remain in prison today. Oscar López Rivera rejected the terms offered by Clinton in 1999 because the offer was not extended to everyone and because it would have required him to serve ten more years on good behavior before being released in a context where guards had already tried to frame him. He is serving fifty-five years on the FALN charges and fifteen for an alleged conspiracy to escape. He was denied parole in 2011; a large-scale international campaign continues to fight for his release through presidential clemency.

Meanwhile, the search for the Macheteros continued. One of the defendants in the Wells Fargo case was Filiberto Ojeda Ríos, a cofounder of the Macheteros and a well-respected fighter in the struggle for Puerto Rican independence. Ojeda Ríos was captured in 1985 after an attack on his house by FBI agents. Following Ojeda Ríos's successful campaign to win bail, with the requirement that he wear an electronic ankle bracelet to monitor his whereabouts, federal authorities—desperate to incarcerate him—charged him with shooting an FBI agent during his arrest. But, in a trial where he represented himself, the Puerto Rican jury accepted his self-defense argument and acquitted him. In 1990, Ojeda Ríos removed his ankle bracelet and once again went underground. The U.S. government then tried him in absentia in Connecticut on the Wells Fargo charges, this time securing a conviction and a fifty-five-year sentence.

In the intervening years, Ojeda Ríos periodically released communiqués from the Macheteros. At the age of seventy-two, he was killed at his rural home by an FBI sniper on September 23, 2005—the fifteenth anniversary of his return to clandestinity. It was also Grito de Lares, a Puerto Rican holiday of resistance. The FBI surrounded his house, opened fire, and denied him medical assistance after shooting him in the neck. He bled to death.

Ojeda Ríos's murder led to large protests and broad calls to investigate the FBI and also kicked off a new wave of repression against the Puerto Rican movement. Five months later, FBI officials raided the homes of several independence activists, and in January 2008 three New York City–based Puerto Ricans in their twenties and thirties were called before grand juries, and two others were subpoenaed later in the year. In February 2008, another alleged Machetero leader, Avelino González Claudio, who had also been living underground for more than twenty years, was arrested in Puerto Rico and extradited to Connecticut to stand trial for the Wells Fargo robbery. In 2011, police arrested his brother, Norberto, for the same charges. In separate trials, both brothers pleaded guilty and have faced a series of health problems during their incarceration. Avelino was freed in February 2013. Norberto is slated for release by 2016.

The 2008 grand jury was a revival of a federal tactic that between 1976 and 1990 had led to numerous activists unaffiliated with the underground—not only Puerto Ricans, but also Chicana/o, Venezuelan, and white North American allies—being subpoenaed to grand juries and, in almost all cases, jailed for refusing to cooperate. The state frequently used the grand jury system as fishing expeditions to fragment the movement and remove vocal supporters of underground actions from public organizing. The government had done this many times since at least the late 1960s. The grand jury repression emanating from the FALN investigations, however, was fiercer. Determined to crush the strong position of noncollaboration with government inquisitions pioneered by Juan Antonio Corretjer in 1936 and pursued by many later independentistas, prosecutors charged several resisters with criminal contempt, which carries an unlimited sentence, as opposed to the eighteen-month maximum for those found in civil contempt. In the end, mass pressure limited the criminal contempt sentences to three years. Grand juries were not only directed against the Puerto Rican movement and its allies: throughout the 1970s and 1980s, dozens of people also served anywhere from weeks to years in prison for refusing to cooperate with grand juries investigating the BLA, American Indian Movement, Weather Underground, and other militant organizations. (In more recent years under the Obama administration, the tactic had been dusted off with new grand juries being used against antiwar activists, ecologists, and anarchists.)

One more aspect of the Puerto Rican anticolonial movement bears mentioning here: the struggle over Vieques. For decades, this tiny island, which is part of Puerto Rico, was used by the U.S. military for weapons training after the Navy appropriated two-thirds of the island in the 1940s. In the late 1970s, after a successful campaign stopped similar war games in the neighboring island of Culebra, the Navy increased its bombing practice on Vieques.

With the support of people and organizations in the United States, including several prominent activists and celebrities, Puerto Rican activists staged a series of blockades and demonstrations against the Navy's presence. The first round of protest occurred between 1978 and 1983, and there was a subsequent spike in activism following the death of Vieques resident David Sanes Rodríguez in April 1999 by two stray bombs. In both phases of the campaign, which succeeded in removing the Navy in 2003, high-risk civil disobedience actions (such as using flotillas to prevent practice bombings) generated several political prisoners. While these sentences were often less than a year, they were disproportionate to the nonviolent nature of the actions.

Furthermore, prison sentences have not been the only risk of working against U.S. militarism in Vieques: In November 1979, while serving a six-month sentence for

trespassing on military land in Vieques as part of a nonviolent mass occupation, La Liga Socialista Puertorriqueña
leader Angel Rodríguez Cristóbal was found beaten to death
and hanged in his jail cell in Florida. A month later, a joint
commando of the Macheteros, OVRP, and CRP opened fire
on a U.S. Navy bus in Puerto Rico, killing two Naval personnel and wounding nine; their communiqué declared that the
action was in response to Rodriguez Cristóbal's murder. His
death confirmed for independence activists, those engaged
in both legal and clandestine organizing, the depths to which
the state would go to crush dissent. And yet it strengthened
their resolve to fight for a free Puerto Rico.

## CHICANO LIBERATION

As with Indigenous and Puerto Rican resistance, the Chicano
movement also displayed great initiative in the late 1960s.
The Chicano liberation movement has always been strongly
rooted in historic Aztlán, the colonized parts of Mexico taken
as part of the 1848 war and which are now the Southwest
United States (Texas, New Mexico, Arizona, and California).
The Chicano movement has taken several forms; catalyzed
by the Black Power movement, organizations like the Brown
Berets formed with a similar program of community-based
revolutionary nationalism. The grassroots struggles of

Chicano youth have been particularly powerful, as students have led walkouts from schools in California and elsewhere in the Southwest against a variety of racist and anti-youth ballot initiatives over the years. The Movimiento Estudiantil Chicano de Aztlán (MEChA) has been a particularly potent force in these struggles—leading Arizona lawmakers to propose a statewide bill in April 2008 that would deny funding to any school with organizations whose membership is based on race.

Led by César Chávez, the United Farm Workers proved an inspiring example of organizing Chicano workers for a decade beginning in the mid-1960s (before descending into a dangerous and divisive cult of personality by the mid-1970s). UFW activists, including Chávez and Dolores Huerta, staged several hunger strikes and other dramatic actions against both corporate farms and government immigration policies, leading them and several of their comrades to serve brief stints in jail for their participation in assorted civil disobedience actions. Meanwhile, and, partly in response to the machismo of male radicals, Chicana feminism became a spearhead of women of color feminism, Cherríe Moraga and Gloria Anzaldúa, editors of *This Bridge Called My Back*, being the best-known examples.

The Chicano movement did not produce an underground the way other movements did, although sectors of the Chicano national liberation movement teamed up with the Puerto Rican independence movement for a time in the 1980s, a coalition that vocally supported clandestine actions by Latino groups. And there is a robust history of militancy and (armed) self-defense within the Chicano movement that, together with the ensuing state repression, has been no less fierce.

Two examples from California testify to the growing militancy of the Chicano movement in the time period in question. On Mayday 1969, seven youth were arrested in the Mission District in San Francisco after an altercation with two plainclothes police officers left one dead. Police reinforcements then arrived, firing automatic weapons and flooding the house with tear gas. The group was dubbed Los Siete de la Raza, despite the fact that the men were of Central American rather than Chicano descent. Still, the case became a rallying cry for Chicano, Latino, and people of color organizations more generally, as the seven were defended by leftist attorneys and supported by a range of radical groups. The defense committees that sprung up to support them became leading entities in Chicano radicalism following their 1971 acquittal.

The other example typifies a Chicano internationalism. On December 20, 1969, about seventy Brown Berets staged an antiwar march in Los Angeles. Eighteen months later, on August 29, 1970, more than twenty thousand Chicanos marched in Los Angeles against the Vietnam War. The Chicano Moratorium March was the largest antiwar demonstration by an oppressed national community in the United States, and it reflected a growing radicalization of Chicanos, particularly young people, connecting the history of U.S. colonialism against Mexico to the war. A broad gathering of progressive and radical Chicanos, the Moratorium signaled a growing movement in which opposition to police brutality was a cornerstone. As was true in Black ghettos and Indigenous reservations, the Mexican barrios viewed the police as an army occupying their communities. The Chicano Moratorium was a community resisting such colonial control.

After a peaceful, joyous march, the protesters were attacked as police charged the park where the rally was concluding. Many of the young people there fought back, lobbing tear gas canisters and rocks back at the police. Dozens were hurt; 150 were arrested in the resulting battles that caused more than $1 million in damage. Most significantly, three were killed: a fifteen-year-old Brown Beret named Lynn Ward was thrown through a plate glass window from an explosion in a trash can, most likely a tear gas canister; Angel Gilberto Díaz was shot in the head while driving; and Ruben Salazar, a sympathetic Chicano journalist who was covering the march for the *Los Angeles Times*, was killed when police stormed into a bar where he and other journalists were sitting after the march. Salazar was killed by a tear gas canister projectile that hit him in the head.

In the face of rampant police violence and a legacy of disenfranchisement, a series of organizations sprouted up to provide political alternatives for Chicano communities at the time. Two of the most famous and most militant were La Alianza Federal de Pueblos Libre and the Crusade for Justice. La Alianza was led by Reies López Tijerina and was in many ways the model for Chicano radicalism. Bridging traditional Chicano land claims with a fighting spirit, La Alianza was founded in 1963 to pursue the treaties the United States had signed after annexing northern Mexico in 1848. The group sought land grants for the Mexican farmers living in northern New Mexico.

Upon its founding, on the anniversary of the 1848 treaty, La Alianza began petitioning the U.S. government for their lands. Not waiting for the American state to accede, La Alianza began reclaiming the land and establishing a governing apparatus. When two forest rangers attempted to evict La Alianza activists in 1966, three hundred people participated in arresting the rangers, trying them in a people's court, and convicting them of trespass. They were released with a suspended sentence. This confident approach became a hallmark of La Alianza, leading to repeated altercations with law enforcement. Tijerina and four others were arrested for the action and ultimately sentenced to between thirty days and two years in prison. But La Alianza was undeterred; Tijerina issued a citizen's arrest warrant, even filing it with the Supreme Court, for Judge Warren Burger when the latter man was appointed by Nixon to head the Supreme Court as a law-and-order justice.

The most famous Alianza action occurred on June 5, 1967. Two days earlier, police had preemptively arrested eleven Alianza activists in an attempt to shut down the organization. In response, Tijerina led an armed raid on the Rio Arriba County Courthouse in Tierra Amarilla, New Mexico. The action was twofold: to free the captured comrades and to place the district attorney under citizen's arrest for the repression. The prosecutor didn't show up, but two officers were shot in the melee. The Alianza activists, including those arrested on June 3, left the courthouse victorious. In response, the governor launched the biggest manhunt in New Mexico's history to capture anyone who participated in the attack. Tijerina eventually turned himself in, serving thirty-five days and using the attention generated from his case to boost Chicano demands. Defending himself at trial, Tijerina was acquitted of all charges in the state case. Upon release, he resumed his organizing activities, becoming a controversial leader in Martin Luther King Jr.'s initiative, the Poor People's Campaign. In 1970, he stood trial in a federal case stemming from the courthouse raid and was sentenced to two years in prison. He was released in 1971 on the condition that he not hold leadership in the Alianza, which soon collapsed.

Through the Crusade for Justice, Denver became an epicenter of the Chicano movement. Rudolfo "Corky" González, who founded the Crusade as a youth conference in 1966, is also credited with having popularized the notion of a distinctly Chicano identity as Indigenous, European, Mexican, and American through his poem "Yo Soy Joaquín." Like Tijerina, González built an organization guided by revolutionary nationalism and a commitment to self-defense. González also became a leader in the Poor People's Campaign; his increasing visibility led the FBI to consider charging him as part of the Chicago conspiracy trial, though they knew he wasn't present during the Democratic National Convention protests. The Crusade held protests against the brutality of police and white supremacists, demonstrated in solidarity with both La Alianza and with Black Power activists, and engaged in a variety of actions opposing the Vietnam War and racism against Chicano high school students. The Crusade occupied Columbus Park, renaming it La Raza.

Given their high profile and militant style, the Crusade found itself increasingly targeted by surveillance and repression. Because the Crusade helped coordinate an impressive Pan-Latino display of solidarity with the Wounded Knee occupation, the FBI suspected it of running guns to AIM and

publicly accused the Crusade of conspiring to kill police officers. In 1973, police arrested a man for jaywalking in front
of an apartment building that served as the Crusade headquarters, sparking a bigger, armed conflagration between
police and the Chicano community. Crusade member Luis
Martínez, twenty, was killed in the fracas that also saw a
dozen police officers injured (four from gunfire). An explosion, which Crusade activists say police set off but which
police say was the Crusade's doing, destroyed much of the
upstairs apartment. City officials had the apartment, and any
evidence therein, destroyed. More than sixty people were
arrested, with four being prosecuted for felony assault.

Police killed several Chicano activists in the Denver area
and beyond, including some associated with the Crusade.
Later in the 1970s, Crusade activists were subpoenaed to
appear before grand juries investigating the FALN. This
repression targeted people throughout the Chicano movement. For instance, Francisco Eugenio "Kiko" Martínez, a
Chicano activist who served as attorney for the Crusade (and
other radical groups), was indicted in 1973 on charges of
mailing three bombs to various targets in Denver. Fearing for
his life, he fled to Mexico but was arrested trying to reenter
the United States in 1980. He then faced separate trials for
each bombing; the first was thrown out after it was discovered that the trial judge had met with prosecutors and witnesses to devise a plan for Martínez's conviction. He was
acquitted at the second trial; charges were dropped in the
third after police destroyed physical evidence. He was ultimately convicted in 1986 for trying to reenter the country
with false identification, though this conviction was overturned on appeal and Martínez was reinstated to the bar.
Others were not so lucky. Six Chicano activists in their twenties and thirties in Boulder were killed in May 1974 when two
car bombs exploded on two successive nights. Police charged
that the two sets of three activists were transporting bombs
that exploded prematurely, though others dispute this claim.
A grand jury was convened on the "Boulder 6" but passed
down no indictments and was not made public.

The most prominent Chicano political prisoner today is Alvaro Luna Hernández. A longtime community organizer in both Houston and Alpine, Texas, Luna Hernández has a history of defending political prisoners; he was the national coordinator of the Ricardo Aldape Guerra Defense Committee, which fought to free a Mexican national who had been sent to Texas's death row on trumped-up charges. Luna Hernández's lengthy political involvement also included his work with the National Movement of La Raza, Stop the Violence Youth Committee, and the Prisoners Solidarity Committee. He spent more than a decade in prison for crimes he did not commit, ultimately being released after newspaper reports helped prove his innocence. He was organizing against police brutality in Chicano communities when an officer came to his house on July 18, 1996, to arrest him on a spurious robbery charge. The officer drew his gun when Luna Hernández questioned his arrest; he disarmed the officer without hurting him and received a fifty-year sentence for "threatening" the officer. He has become a valuable and successful jailhouse lawyer since his incarceration.

Alvaro Luna Hernández

# Anti-imperialism, Anti-authoritarianism, and Revolutionary Nonviolence

**2**

## THE POLITICS OF SOLIDARITY

As illustrated above, militancy became an increasingly pervasive phenomenon among the U.S. Left by the end of the 1960s, with some pushing for coordinated armed struggle. The sector of the Left that was predominantly white followed a somewhat similar trajectory, though its roots and development differed in key ways.

The biggest and most famous, primarily white New Left organization of the 1960s was Students for a Democratic Society, a youth- and student-based group that had an estimated membership of one hundred thousand people by the time it collapsed in 1969. Originally the student wing of the anticommunist social democratic League for Industrial Democracy, SDS became an independent and multitendency organization in 1962. It was particularly catalyzed by the Student Nonviolent Coordinating Committee and the civil rights movement, as well as the war in Vietnam. SDS sponsored the first antiwar march in 1965, which brought twenty thousand people to Washington, DC. The group continued to grow exponentially throughout the decade, becoming home to assorted radicals broadly united in opposition to war and racism and celebration of counterculture. The reasons for its collapse were varied, but included unbridgeable fissures over organizational strategy and direction amid what seemed to many a revolutionary era.

Out of SDS's collapse emerged many groups, including the Weatherman, later the Weather Underground. Taking its name from a line in a Bob Dylan song ("you don't need a weatherman to know which way the wind blows"), the Weather Underground included some of the best-known SDS leaders at the time, articulated a politics that defined Black people and other people of color as colonized populations, and saw the role of white people as opening another front of struggle in the fight against imperialism. Such militant solidarity, argued Weather, would overextend the state and its ability to repress revolutionary struggles and therefore hasten the pace and success of revolutions around the globe.

Weatherman was the most visible, vocal, and organized expression of white Left militancy, but it was far from the only one. One month after Weather led a few hundred people in a violent demonstration in Chicago, ten thousand people during an antiwar protest formed a breakaway march to trash the U.S. Justice Department. A significant minority of New Leftists were turning to bombs, targeting banks and recruiting stations, while many more fought back against police at demonstrations and called for armed struggle. A map of the United States printed in a (temporarily censored) 1971 special issue of the radical *Scanlan's Monthly* on guerrilla war listed thousands of acts of political violence between 1965 and 1970; according to journalist Kirkpatrick Sale, from September 1969 to May 1970, there was at least one bombing or attempted bombing somewhere in the United States every day by the progressive and radical movements. Communities of color were often the most militant, as evidenced by the ghetto rebellions of the mid-1960s, but by the end of the decade many white radicals were also joining in the fray.

Some such expressions of militancy were more organized than others. A New York City cell organized by a man named Sam Melville bombed several targets in 1969: an induction center, two banks, two corporate headquarters, a courthouse, and the federal building. The group was set up by an FBI informant, and several of its members were arrested. The main person to stand trial, Melville died when police violently crushed the Attica prison rebellion. His partner and collaborator, Jane Alpert, skipped bail and lived underground for several years before turning herself in and cooperating with the state.

In Madison, Wisconsin, a small group calling itself the New Year's Gang bombed an on-campus army research facility in August 1970. Although they had taken precautions to avoid injury, a postdoctoral student working late into the night was killed in the blast. A month later, a Boston bank robbery intended to fund further clandestine activities, and carried out with weapons expropriated from a National Guard armory, went awry when the radicals killed a police officer. Susan Saxe and Kathy Power fled the scene and remained underground for years. The two Brandeis students—Saxe had graduated the previous spring, Power was still enrolled at the time of the robbery—had teamed up with three former prisoners to commit the robbery. Two of them, Stanley Bond and William Gilday, were captured shortly after the robbery and would end up dying in prison—Bond in 1972 during a failed attempt to escape, Gilday in 2011 of Parkinson's disease. Saxe received significant support from the lesbian feminist community, bridging antiwar militancy with the burgeoning radical women's movement as several women went to jail rather than cooperate with grand juries investigating her whereabouts. Captured unrepentant in 1975, Saxe served eight years. Power stayed underground until 1993, when she turned herself in, expressed contrition, and served six years in prison.

Although Weather had been the most vocal adherent of armed struggle, its path changed in March 1970, when three members of the group died when a bomb they were building exploded. Because that bomb had been intended for human targets, the deaths compelled the Weather leadership to declare that the group would continue to pursue a clandestine strategy but one that would refrain from causing any injury. It changed its name to the Weather Underground, deepened the clandestine infrastructure it had developed, and at its best moments looked to engage creatively with aboveground struggles rather than act as vanguard. Over the next seven years, the group claimed credit for more than two dozen bombings of high-profile targets such as the Pentagon, numerous courthouses and police stations, the U.S. Agency for International Development, and several corporations involved in the coup in Chile or colonialism in Angola. Weather articulated a politics of solidarity that demanded a high level of sacrifice by whites in support of Black and other revolutionary people of color. This support emanated from a strategic belief, pioneered by Che Guevara, that U.S. imperialism could be defeated through overextension; bombings were an attempt to pierce the myth of government invincibility and draw repressive attention away from the Panthers and similar groups. It also reflected a political position that said white people had to side with Third World struggles against the U.S. government—and had to do so in a similarly dramatic way.

The end of the Vietnam War, which dried up some of Weather's hippie base, brought a crisis of direction. With the Black and Native liberation movements facing stiff repression, with the Puerto Rican independence movement gaining traction, with the National Liberation Front of Vietnam emerging victorious against U.S. colonialism, and with much less motion among white Americans, the Weather Underground was lost. Through its aboveground support organization, the Prairie Fire Organizing Committee, Weather initiated the Hard Times conference in 1976. The conference brought a

multiracial group of approximately two thousand people to Chicago—where it then fell apart, as various Black and women's groups present sharply criticized its agenda, which they saw as significantly diluted from the approach that had been Weather's calling card. The failure of the conference brought other internal contradictions to light, and the group was torn apart amid bitter factionalism in 1976–1977. A group calling itself the Revolutionary Committee of the Weather Underground expelled the Central Committee and attempted to rebuild armed struggle but was caught in an FBI sting operation. Five people served between two to four years as a result.

The end of Weather was significant, but it did not signal the end of armed struggle among white radicals. Most people in the group surfaced, especially after the Revolutionary Committee busts. Upon surfacing, people generally found their way to other radical groups, especially the Prairie Fire Organizing Committee (PFOC), which had been formed in 1975 to provide public support for Weather's politics and clandestine actions. PFOC was also rocked by the failure of Hard Times, with a shakeup of leadership—especially after one of the leaders was arrested for being part of the Revolutionary Committee.

In 1980, a group of West Coast Prairie Fire activists (including a former member of Weather) went underground in an attempt to continue armed struggle and help some political prisoners escape. They were unsuccessful, but eluded capture until turning themselves in to police in 1994. Two people, Claude Marks and Donna Willmott, served several years in prison.

On the East Coast, the PFOC maintained a stronger relationship with the Black liberation movement, particularly with the seeming revival of the BLA in the late 1970s. A split, born more of sectarian infighting than substantive political differences, tore PFOC apart; while the group on the West Coast kept the name, the New York City group became the May 19th Communist Organization, named after the birthdate of Malcolm X and Ho Chi Minh. May 19th was small and severe; it had significant lesbian leadership and employed a variety of strategies to aid Third World liberation struggles in the United States and abroad. The group pledged its support to the BLA and various Third World liberation struggles, and it, too, led many militant demonstrations in which activists faced off with police. While it had long been the subject of police harassment as a result of its protests—several people served jail time for a militant demonstration against the South African Springboks rugby team's 1980 U.S. tour, for instance, and the group was no stranger to physically standing off against police—May 19th was ultimately crushed by the wave of repression that followed the failed Brink's robbery in 1981.

As we have seen, on October 20, 1981, a BLA unit working with white supporters attempted to rob a Brink's armored car. Arrested at the scene of the failed, tragic robbery were two former members of the Weather Underground—Kathy Boudin, who had remained underground, and David Gilbert, who had returned underground—as well as Judy Clark, who was a public activist and known leader of May 19th. Indeed, Clark was a lead plaintiff in the lawsuit May 19th helped file with New Afrikan leader Mutulu Shakur against the FBI for COINTELPRO. Clark's arrest brought immense pressure on May 19th activists and supporters, along with numerous Black activists, who were harassed, intimidated, arrested, and called before grand juries in the three years following Brink's. As mentioned earlier, some of those charged were ultimately exonerated, while others went to jail. The longest sentence for the aboveground white activists—forty years—was given to May 19th leader Silvia Baraldini (along with her codefendant, BLA member Sekou Odinga) in the 1983 RICO case. The following year, Baraldini was given an additional three years, along with Puerto Rico solidarity activist Shelley Miller, for resisting a grand jury investigating the Puerto Rican independence movement. An Italian national, Baraldini fought to be repatriated to her home country. After a long campaign by her and her supporters, including a large movement in Italy, she was returned there in 1999 and set free in 2006.

The climate of constant arrests and intimidation follow-ing the Brink's fiasco put May 19th on the defensive as it tried to protect itself and support those incarcerated. Several of the group's active members felt unable to continue work-ing politically as they had been, and as a result they went underground. Others joined them, trying to raise the level of struggle or hoping to deflect the repression against Black and Puerto Rican clandestine groups by mounting additional actions.

Operating in cells alternately called Red Guerrilla Resistance and the Armed Resistance Unit, these group-ings were responsible for more than half a dozen bombings between 1983 and 1985 against U.S. military installations (a DC military base and a navy yard), the U.S. Capitol, the New York offices of Israeli Aircraft Industries, the South African consulate, and the Patrolmen's Benevolent Association. These actions were done in opposition to rampant police murder in Black communities, U.S. imperialism in Latin America and support for apartheid, the invasion of Grenada, and Israeli attacks on Palestine and Lebanon.

While these actions contributed to a climate of militant opposition under Reagan's rule, the newly bolstered security forces clamped down on the persisting underground. Susan Rosenberg and Tim Blunk were arrested in November 1984, and Alan Berkman, Marilyn Buck, Linda Evans, and Laura Whitehorn were arrested in May 1985. All except Buck had previously been involved in May 19th, working in public formations such as the John Brown Anti-Klan Committee against police brutality, South African apart-heid, and white supremacy and in the New Movement in Solidarity with Puerto Rican Independence and Socialism. (Years before, Evans and Whitehorn had also been members of Weather.) Buck had long supported the Black liberation struggle in a variety of formations; in 1973 she had been arrested and sentenced to ten years for purchasing two boxes of bullets, which the government alleged were for the Black Liberation Army. She had been wanted since 1977, when she was let out from federal prison on furlough and never returned.

Arrested at a storage unit where they had been keeping explosives, Blunk and Rosenberg were tried on charges of weapons and explosives possession and given an unprecedented sentence of fifty-eight years. (By comparison, Michael Donald Bray, who in the 1980s was active in the far-right "Army of God," served less than four years for bombing ten occupied abortion clinics and offices of the ACLU.) Berkman was jailed for a year in 1982 for resisting a grand jury; a doctor, he went underground rather than face trial on charges of providing medical care to Marilyn Buck while she was underground. He was ultimately convicted of possession of weapons, explosives and false IDs, as well as bail jumping, and sentenced to twelve years. Evans received thirty-five years for illegally obtaining handguns and false IDs, and for harboring Buck. Whitehorn, held for more than two years in "preventive detention," was convicted of possession of false IDs and contempt of court.

Besides facing individual charges emanating from the circumstances of their arrest, the six were subsequently indicted together as part of what became known as the Resistance Conspiracy case. They were charged with "conspiracy to oppose, protest, and change the policies and practices of the U.S. government in domestic and international matters by violent and illegal means." On top of the lengthy sentences most of them were already serving, this conspiracy charge covered many of the bombings claimed by the Armed Resistance Unit and Red Guerrilla Resistance. In 1990, to secure a faster release for Berkman, who was being denied adequate medical care for a life-threatening recurrence of Hodgkin's lymphoma, Buck, Evans, and Whitehorn pleaded guilty to various charges, including the Capitol bombing; conspiracy charges against Berkman, Blunk, and Rosenberg were dropped. Berkman was released on parole in 1992. His health improved upon release, and he worked as an AIDS doctor and activist, cofounding the Global AIDS Project, Health GAP, an international organization that greatly expanded access to life-saving HIV medications. His cancer returned, however, and he passed away in 2009.

Whitehorn, sentenced to twenty additional years, served a total of fourteen years (counting her earlier jail time) and was released in 1999, jumping back into the AIDS movement and working to free political prisoners. Blunk was released on parole in 1996. A campaign pressuring Bill Clinton to pardon Leonard Peltier and other political prisoners before Clinton left office did not win Peltier's release, though he did grant clemency to Evans and Rosenberg; they were released on his last day in office in 2001.

Buck, meanwhile, was the subject of several trials in the 1980s. In addition to the ten years she received in the Resistance Conspiracy case, she was already serving time from previous trials relating to the Brink's robbery and Assata Shakur's escape. All told, Buck was sentenced to eighty years in prison. She was, however, granted parole and given a date for release. Before it could happen, though, Buck developed an aggressive form of uterine cancer in prison. She was granted compassionate release and embraced by a wide community of friends, family, and comrades. She died on August 2, 2010, three weeks after being freed from prison.

*Laura Whitehorn, Susan Rosenberg, and Marilyn Buck*
*in Dublin women's prison, 1993.*

Shoul

*The Ohio 7 awaiting trial. Standing: Richard Williams, Tom Manning, Ray Luc Levasseur. Seated: Jaan Laaman, Barbara Curzi-Laamaon, Carol Manning, Pat-Gros Levasseur.*

## MILITANTS OF THE WHITE WORKING CLASS

The use of conspiracy charges was a particularly potent tool against political militancy in the 1980s. Besides the cases outlined above, RICO charges were ultimately used against accused members of one of the other primary clandestine organizations of the period: the United Freedom Front (UFF). Unlike many of the other white people discussed above, those accused of belonging to the United Freedom Front came from solidly working-class backgrounds. (While the Weather Underground is sometimes disparaged as the offspring of the bourgeoisie, the class background of its members mirrored that of the dominant sectors of the white New Left overall: some poor, some rich, but overwhelmingly middle class in background.)

The UFF claimed credit for nineteen bombings in the Northeast in the 1980s against assorted U.S. military installations and corporate headquarters, such as General Electric, Motorola, and IBM. These actions were done expressly in solidarity with the revolutionary struggles against racism and U.S. imperialism in El Salvador, Nicaragua, and South

Africa. The UFF took precautions to ensure that no one was killed in any of its bombing attacks; like most other groups, it relied on bank robberies to secure funding for its activities.

Police ultimately charged Barbara Curzi Laaman, Patricia Gros Levasseur, Jaan Laaman, Ray Luc Levasseur, Carol Manning, Tom Manning, and Richard Williams with participation in the UFF. Ray Levasseur and Tom Manning were both Vietnam veterans and accused of previously participating in a similar group called the Sam Melville-Jonathan Jackson Unit. Each of the men had spent time in prison in the late 1960s or early 1970s, for drugs or apolitical robberies—not unheard of circumstances for veterans and other working-class men—which became formative experiences in their political development. By 1971, all of them had committed themselves to revolutionary politics. This included, centrally, working with prisoners and their families, supporting Black resistance movements domestically and in South Africa, and joining with other antiwar soldiers. Levasseur ran a radical bookstore in Portland, Maine, which served as a hub for many of these activities. Facing increased repression personally and through the bookstore, Levasseur went underground by 1974. Curzi Laaman, Laaman, and Williams, along with New Afrikan activist Kazi Toure, helped organize the 1979 Amandla concert against apartheid featuring Bob Marley, among others. But repression and the desire to build a movement away from the eyes and ears of the state forced all of them underground by 1981.

On November 4, 1984, federal agents captured Curzi Laaman, Laaman, Gros Levasseur, Levasseur, and Williams in Ohio. The following year, Carol and Tom Manning were captured. Tried together, they were dubbed the Ohio 7, although legal battles took some of them from Ohio to New York, New Jersey, and Massachusetts. These legal battles weren't the only troubles greeting these revolutionaries: except for Williams, whose wife and children did not accompany him underground, the other six were couples who lived and raised their families underground. After the arrest, the government attempted to use the nine children, most of them under ten and all of them minors, as bargaining chips against their parents. The state offered the Levasseurs' eight-year-old daughter $20 and some pizza to cooperate with the government against her family. The Mannings' children were held incommunicado for two months after the parents were first arrested; they had to go on hunger strike to force the government to disclose the whereabouts of their children.

As with the Brink's case, the severity of the charges and the intensity of the search for the accused led to multiple court cases. In assorted trials, all of the Ohio 7, along with Kazi Toure, were convicted on bombing charges: Pat Gros Levasseur received a five-year sentence for harboring a fugitive, her husband; Barbara Curzi Laaman and Carol Manning each received sentences of fifteen years. Ray Luc Levasseur and Richard Williams were sentenced to forty-five years each for their role in UFF bombings, and Jaan Laaman received a sentence of fifty-three years. Besides a fifty-three-year sentence for bombing charges, Tom Manning was sentenced to life in prison during an additional trial for the 1981 self-defense shooting death of a New Jersey trooper. Even though Tom Manning admitted shooting the trooper, claiming he opened fire only after being fired upon, the state of New Jersey also tried Richard Williams for the murder. It took two trials, but Williams was ultimately sentenced to thirty-five years to life on the murder charge. In two separate trials, Kazi Toure was sentenced to eleven years for gun possession (six years on federal charges, up to five years on state charges) and seven years for "seditious conspiracy."

In 1989, after all members of the Ohio 7 had already been convicted on other charges, the government recharged Gros Levasseur, Levasseur, and Williams with racketeering and seditious conspiracy—functionally a charge of treason and gangsterism. Despite the state spending $10 million and calling more than two hundred witnesses, the jury acquitted the defendants of sedition, and the court was forced to drop the RICO charges when the jury could not reach a verdict on them. Barbara Curzi Laaman, Carol Manning, and Pat Gros Levasseur were all released in the 1990s, as was Kazi

Toure. Ray Levasseur was paroled in 2004. After being put in isolation after the September 11 attacks, Richard Williams suffered increasing medical problems. He died in prison in December 2005.

Jaan Laaman and Tom Manning remain in prison. Although he suffers from injuries and medical neglect, Manning continues to paint. Laaman is the founding editor of *4Struggle* magazine, a revolutionary (mostly) online journal of and for political prisoners and their allies (www.4strugglemag.org).

The UFF was not the first clandestine organization composed primarily of white working-class revolutionaries. Indeed, the West Coast political scene in the 1970s, especially in and around Seattle, yielded several insurrectionary underground actions. To be sure, this region contributed more than a few members and supporters of the Weather Underground and its aboveground support groups, but it also bred more local expressions of clandestine militancy, informed by a more anarchist (if still strongly Marxist and generally eclectic) orientation.

The best-known group to emerge out of this milieu was the George Jackson Brigade (GJB). Named after the murdered Black Panther and imprisoned intellectual, the GJB brought together seven militants from the Seattle area. The group had explicitly queer leadership—Bo Brown achieved a degree of notoriety as "the gentleman bank robber" for her daring drag expropriations—and was multiracial due to the involvement of Mark Cook, an ex-Panther and former prisoner who had helped organize inspiring and effective protests from behind prison walls. The group took responsibility for about ten bombings, together with bank robberies to fund their activities and a daring prison escape. More so than any of the armed struggle groups made up (primarily) of white people, the George Jackson Brigade provided clear, armed underground support to labor struggles domestic to the United States, often local to the Pacific Northwest. The group was still internationalist—for instance, it bombed a BMW dealership in protest of the 1977 murders of Red Army Faction leaders in Germany—but its actions were designed primarily to support rebelling prisoners and striking workers in Washington State. The group bombed the Washington Department of Corrections, the corporate offices of the Safeway grocery store chain during a labor dispute, two banks, the state capitol, and several targets connected to the demands of striking autoworkers. Like many other clandestine formations at the time, the Brigade took its media seriously, releasing communiqués explaining their actions as well as statements of support or clarification to unions, poems in honor of captured comrades, and political tracts outlining its practice, beliefs, and (self)criticisms. The Brigade's political statement included essays upholding anarchism and Marxism-Leninism, and it tried to dialogue with other radicals based on its commitment to a variety of Left schools of thought.

Coming almost entirely from working-class backgrounds and with repeated personal run-ins with the law, members of the George Jackson Brigade were as reliant on bank expropriations as the Black Liberation Army and United Freedom Front. During its first attempt in January 1976, police quickly arrived and opened fire on the members inside, killing Bruce Siedel and wounding John Sherman. Ed Mead was also captured at the scene and spent the next eighteen years in prison, becoming a bold jailhouse lawyer, a prolific author, and an organizer of the first Men Against Sexism prison chapter to combat rape and sexual slavery inside. Other members of the Brigade carried out a daring rescue of Sherman from a prison hospital on March 8, 1976, wounding a police officer in the process. This action ultimately landed Brigadista Mark Cook, new to the group and the only nonwhite member, in prison for thirty years—by far the longest anyone served for Brigade actions. Between November 1977 and March 1978, the remaining members of the Brigade were arrested. All served some time in prison and were released between the mid-1980s and 2000s.

Most revolutionaries in this time period, especially those engaged in armed struggle, identified prisons as a bulwark of state repression. As such, radicals pledged their solidarity with prison struggles, often leading to a revolving door between incarceration and revolutionary activities. Prison became both a breeding ground for and a target of insurgency. All of the groups discussed above—the Black Liberation Army, FALN, AIM, the Weather Underground, United Freedom Front, George Jackson Brigade, and dozens of other organizations—directed their actions in various ways against prisons as a fundamental site of racist and ruling-class exploitation. But it was not just formalized groups who targeted the prison system.

On August 21, 1971—the same day George Jackson was murdered—anarchist Larry Giddings was arrested in Los Angeles with a small group attempting to secure weapons for revolutionary action. He was paroled in 1978, at which point he moved to the Bay Area and began working with a radical collective doing prisoner support, among other activities. Released from parole in 1979, Giddings resumed clandestine activities, this time in Seattle, with other antiauthoritarians, including Bill Dunne, a former airplane mechanic. The two were arrested in October 1979 attempting to free a jailed comrade who was killed in the melee. At trial, the pair was also charged with using bank robberies and stolen weapons to carry out the attack. Although he was subject to the post-9/11 temporary disappearance many political prisoners in federal institutions faced, Giddings was paroled in 2004. Dunne, who was sentenced to ninety years at trial plus fifteen years for an attempted escape in 1983, remains incarcerated in supermaximum prisons without much hope of release.

The Jericho Movement

*Bill Dunne*

Harvey Richards Media Archive / estuarypress.com

# REVOLUTIONARY NONVIOLENCE

Although armed actions have been the most dramatic, revolutionary militancy has never been limited to guns and bombs. Hundreds of political prisoners have come from pacifist circles, both secular and religious. While these activists are generally imprisoned on shorter sentences than those described above, their political actions are no less vital, their commitments no less revolutionary. Just as those who engaged in armed struggle never comprised the majority of the movements from which they came, most nonviolent activists who serve prison time for acts of civil disobedience are not revolutionaries. Yet many of them are, and their work provides a vital point through which to build strategic unity among those who differ on questions of tactics. It was, in fact, revolutionary nonviolent activists who maintained dialogue and critical support for armed revolutionaries in the 1970s when other sectors of the Left, who were often theoretically supportive of armed struggle in Third World countries, were decidedly hostile to its domestic iterations.

Beginning in the late 1960s, some activists managed to establish illegal, clandestine structures committed to nonviolent action. While no one knows for sure, it is believed that persons affiliated with this tendency were responsible for the break-in at the Media, Pennsylvania, FBI office that led to the exposure of COINTELPRO. This nonviolent underground had several expressions to aid those in danger: the two most common were to help ferry draft resisters and antiwar soldiers out of the country and to provide safe abortions for women in need before the practice was legalized in 1973. In the 1980s, much of this infrastructure was revived and expanded to provide sanctuary for refugees fleeing repressive, U.S.-backed military regimes in Latin America.

The experiences of these nonviolent revolutionaries disentangle militancy from violence and violence from clandestinity. After all, Dave Dellinger—who served time for resisting conscription in World War II—was the only one of the Chicago 8 defendants to intervene when police bound and gagged Panther leader Bobby Seale during the infamous conspiracy case in 1969, despite the fact that the other defendants were much more publicly in favor of militant confrontation. Likewise, Dellinger was among the most prominent of a small group of older pacifist radicals who continued to maintain a public dialogue with members of the Weather Underground and other militants throughout the 1970s and beyond.

Such militancy also manifested itself in clandestine actions. Perhaps the most famous nonviolent militants of the time were Daniel and Philip Berrigan, Jesuit priests and tested pacifist warriors. The Berrigan brothers and seven other Catholic leftists burned almost four hundred draft files in Catonsville, Maryland, on May 17, 1968, using homemade napalm to protest its widespread use in Vietnam. Regarding the attack, Daniel Berrigan said, "Our apologies, good friends, for the fracture of good order, the burning of paper instead of children, the angering of the orderlies in the front parlor of the charnel house. We could not, so help us God, do otherwise."

All of the Catonsville 9, as they were known, were convicted of destroying government property and interfering with the Selective Service Act. Catonsville was not the first time Catholic leftists had destroyed draft files; a year earlier, Catonsville 9 activists Philip Berrigan and Thomas

Lewis, along with two others, had ruined hundreds of draft records in Baltimore by pouring blood over them. (They were, in fact, out on bail but sentenced to serve six years for this action when they went to the Catonsville draft board.) The Catonsville attack, however, raised the stakes through the use of arson. "We do this because everything else has failed," one of the defendants said during the action itself.

The Catonsville fire helped spark a more militant style of antiwar protest, as thousands of radicals, religious and secular alike, began attacking draft offices and destroying draft files. Catholic leftists found themselves facing political trials for their stiff resistance to the war, including the outlandish charge against seven pacifists (including Philip Berrigan and his wife, Elizabeth McAlister) for supposedly conspiring to kidnap Henry Kissinger in 1972.

The Catonsville action upped the ante in another way as well: after being convicted and sentenced to serve two to three years, five of the nine went underground rather than go to jail. Most of those who went underground did not stay long, either turning themselves in or being captured. Three days after releasing an audiotaped message of solidarity and constructive criticism to the Weather Underground, one of many public statements he made while underground, Daniel Berrigan was arrested in August 1970. But Mary Moylan, a former nun, evaded capture altogether. She eventually joined the Weather Underground, pursuing a clandestine strategy until 1978, when the group had fallen apart and she turned herself in to serve a three-year sentence from the Catonsville action.

This sector of the Catholic Left—with roots dating back to Dorothy Day and the Catholic Worker Movement, as well as the War Resisters League, World War II draft resistance, and bohemian anarchist circles of the 1950s—has continued organizing against empire. This has included everything from war tax resistance to attempts at shutting down the School of the Americas counterinsurgency training center to ongoing civil disobedience against U.S. wars. Whereas political prisoners of the armed-struggle Left are often distinguished by serving lengthy sentences, radical pacifists are more known for the sheer number of times they find themselves behind bars for civil disobedience. For more than forty years, it has been the political tendency most oriented toward civil disobedience, and adherents have served sentences of several months to several years for resisting the apparatuses of war through nonviolent confrontation, including direct action.

In 1980, the Berrigan brothers helped found the Plowshares movement, which became one of the best-known expressions of radical pacifism in the decade. The name comes from an injunction in the Bible, to "beat swords into plowshares"—that is, convert weapons of war to peaceful uses or get rid of them altogether. It was a movement targeting the use and proliferation of nuclear power and weapons. In the first Plowshares action, eight activists went to a General Electric plant in King of Prussia, Pennsylvania, poured blood on documents, and destroyed missile reentry nose cones designed for a first-strike nuclear system. Activists affiliated with the Plowshares movement were responsible for at least thirty actions throughout the decade. At the height of the Cold War arms race, Plowshares activists dismantled nuclear weapons, submarines, helicopters, and other military equipment, often with implements as simple as a common hammer and by pouring their own blood over the weapons. Their actions were effective at literally dismantling instruments of the military.

Unlike others who carried out high-risk actions, Plowshares activists did not adopt a hit-and-run strategy. Their project was one of moral and spiritual witness. As such, they awaited their capture at the scene of an action, using the trial and surrounding publicity, even jail time, as further opportunity to spread their political message. During these trials, Plowshares activists and other pacifists (including, for instance, those who engaged in antiwar civil disobedience during Gulf Wars I and II) have cited international law and the necessity defense as justification for their actions—sometimes resulting in lower sentences or even acquittals. While most Plowshares activists came from a religious background, the antinuclear and antiauthoritarian politics were also salient; for instance, Jewish secular anarchofeminist Katya Komisaruk dismantled a military computer designed to guide nuclear missiles as part of her involvement in Plowshares. She served five years in prison.

The average Plowshares sentence has hovered around two years in prison, although several activists have received longer sentences. The longest Plowshares sentence occurred in Missouri for four activists who used a jackhammer and air compressor to damage the cover lid of a missile silo at an air force base in 1984. Larry Cloud Morgan received an eight-year sentence; Paul Kabat, ten years; Helen Woodson, eighteen years; and Carl Kabat, who had participated in two earlier Plowshares actions, eighteen years. Morgan and Woodson's sentences were reduced on appeal, though both still served years in prison. Plowshares actions continue, albeit with less regularity.

Revolutionary nonviolence in the 1970s and 1980s over-lapped considerably with radical feminism, especially lesbian feminism. The Women's Pentagon Actions in 1980 and 1981 attempted to use civil disobedience to shut down the heart of American militarism, and there were dozens of such actions at weapons plants and military offices across the country. Many of these organizers, including Barbara Deming, one of the best-known theorists and practitioners of revolution-ary nonviolence, helped build the 1983 Seneca Women's Encampment for a Future of Justice and Peace. The camp, which involved thousands of women challenging imperi-alism and militarism as patriarchal endeavors, attempted to stop the deployment of nuclear weapons from a nearby army depot. The camp was both an intentional community of feminists, including many lesbians, and a constant exercise in civil disobedience. Fifty-four women were arrested when Marines attempted to break up the camp. It was disbanded after four months. There was a similar encampment in the Puget Sound at this time.

Since the War on Terror, revolutionary nonviolence has reemerged in the case of several draft resisters and active-duty soldiers challenging U.S. empire—starting, perhaps, with Stephen Eagle Funk, a gay Filipino man who refused to deploy to Iraq and became a leading member of Iraq Veterans Against the War. The best-known political prisoner to come from this milieu is Chelsea (formerly known as Bradley) Manning, a young Army intelligence analyst deployed to Iraq who was arrested in 2010 on suspicion of having leaked a bevy of classified materials to the antisecrecy WikiLeaks organization after failing to interest the mainstream media in the materials. The hundreds of thousands of leaked documents—the largest such forced declassification in history—included video footage of massacres in Afghanistan and Iraq, as well as hundreds of thousands of diplomatic cables and army reports. Manning was a gay-identified soldier who became an opponent of the Iraq war after learning of U.S. massacres and support for Iraq government torture. For nine months of pretrial detention, Manning was held in extreme isolation and subjected to what the UN Rapporteur on Torture deemed "cruel, inhuman, and degrading treatment." Initially facing the death penalty, and then life in prison, Manning pleaded guilty to ten of the charges in a military tribunal in February 2013. Six months later, the military judge convicted Manning of twenty charges total—mostly for espionage, theft and fraud—and imposed a sentence of thirty-five years in prison and a dishonorable discharge from

*Mural honoring Chelsea Manning in Williamsburg, Brooklyn.*

the military. Manning came out as transgender the day after being sentenced, saying her name is Chelsea Manning and asking supporters to use her chosen name and female pronouns (except, as she put it, "in official mail to the confinement facility").

Though Manning was acquitted of the "aiding the enemy" charge that carried the possible life sentence, her conviction and long sentence were a stiff message to activists seeking transparency of information. Indeed, the Obama administration has charged seven people for leaking classified information—more than double the number of prosecuted leaks in any other presidential administration. The latest, Edward Snowden, was a government contractor who was charged with releasing thousands of documents about massive electronic spying by the National Security Agency; he remains in exile. Other independent journalists and information activists, including Jeremy Hammond and Barrett Brown, have also faced stiff penalties for their efforts to expose spying by the U.S. government and cybersecurity agencies. Brown was still awaiting trial at the end of 2013. Hammond, affiliated with the hacker network Anonymous, was sentenced in November 2013 to ten years for hacking into the computer files of a private security firm named Stratfor that had spied on a variety of activist groups. Hammond's actions, which destroyed some of Stratfor's technological capacities and redirected their money to philanthropic donations, were led and overseen by an FBI informant.

Next to Manning, one of the most high-profile cases involving the prosecution of computer activists was that of Aaron Swartz, a critic of the privatization of knowledge through copyright. A prominent activist in support of internet access and openness, he was arrested by MIT police in 2011 for having made freely available thousands of scholarly articles copyright protected by university databases. Facing thirty-five years in prison and $1 million in fines, the twenty-six-year-old Swartz hanged himself in January 2013.

Militant Catholic leftists, anarchist-pacifists, radical feminists, and other nonviolent activists helped rewrite the script of radical action—making it both politically deeper and more fun. Radicals affiliated with these tendencies valued direct democracy as well as direct action. They emphasized anarchist organizing processes: decentralized, consensus-based affinity groups were the model of action. This style helped inform the actions that shut down of the World Trade Organization in Seattle in November 1999 and subsequent global justice demonstrations. But the fusion of anarchism, spirituality, and direct action expressed itself well before then. Since the 1980s, perhaps the most visible expression of this approach came from the environmental movement.

JUDI BARI 1949-1997

MAXXAM

ENVIRONMENTALISTS AND LOGGERS UNITE!

"A revolutionary ecology movement must also organize among poor and working people. With the exception of the toxics movement and the native land rights movement most U.S. environmentalists are white and privileged. This group is too invested in the system to pose it much of a threat. A revolutionary ideology in the hands of privileged people can indeed bring about some disruption and change in the system. But a revolutionary ideology in the hands of working people can bring that system to a halt. For it is the working people who have their hands on the machinery. And only by stopping the machinery of destruction can we ever hope to stop this madness."

CELEBRE LA HISTORIA POPULAR
CELEBRATE PEOPLES HISTORY
CELEBRER DE L'HISTOIRE DES GENS

Poster by Nicolas Lampert, POBox 1090, Milwaukee, WI 53201 • For more posters: www.justseeds.org • Photo by Evan Johnson, www.judibari.org

Nicolas Lampert / Justseeds

# Earth and Animal Liberation

THE 1970S INAUGURATED MANY THINGS, INCLUDING THE FIRST EARTH DAY CELEBRATION, ON April 22, 1970. While the celebration has, by and large, become just another kitschy, corporate-sponsored festival, it also signals a growing concern with environmentalism and sustainability. The interest in protecting the earth and its resources has found many expressions in recent decades, ranging from communal living and recycling to civil disobedience and sabotage. All of these activities, in fact, have increased as scientists, farmers, and others around the world call attention to the crisis of global climate change.

While liberal nonprofits attempted to steer the new-found environmental concern to more watered-down ends, radical environmentalists began to congregate around a group and political framework called Earth First! (EF!). Inspired in part by the "ecotage" novels of Edward Abbey, EF! formed in 1979–1980 in the Southwest under the banner "No Compromise in Defense of Mother Earth." Behind its single focus on the environment, the group brought together a politically diverse range of activists, including some reactionary and even racist elements in its earlier years. By the mid-1980s, tensions between reactionaries and others were causing more and more conflicts within the organization, until a 1990 split led to the group being grounded more firmly in the anarchist milieu. While formally rejecting the state, EF! politics have tended to target corporate power as the greatest threat to environmental sustainability.

Activists associated with Earth First! have been responsible for direct-action environmentalism against logging, dam and other hazardous development, pollution, and genetic engineering. It has embraced a direct-action and, since 1990, more explicitly anarchist organizing style and placed high value on tree sits, roadblocks, and monkeywrenching. Indeed, many credit Earth First! with helping develop a variety of creative forms of civil disobedience that are both high profile and successful.

The best-known target of government repression against EF! was Judi Bari, a former labor organizer turned environmentalist. More than anyone else, Bari bridged environmental and economic concerns—a vital task at a time when the timber industry tried to position economic necessity as the reason for deforestation. Bari flipped the script, organizing workers and environmentalists to seize corporate property and eliminate corporate power. Bari also added a strong feminist presence to Earth First! leadership and activism, helping to displace the negative image the group had developed in the 1980s.

With the help of Earth First! troubadour Darryl Cherney, Bari organized Redwood Summer in 1990, an effort self-consciously indebted to SNCC's Mississippi Summer in 1964 and similarly attempting to bring thousands of young people and national attention to fight for justice—this time, California's redwood forests. While organizing for the summer program in Oakland in May 1990, a bomb placed under the driver's seat in Bari's car exploded, shattering her pelvis and wounding Cherney. Three hours later, while still at the hospital, Bari and Cherney were placed under arrest, as local and federal law enforcement agents said the pair were terrorists and were the only suspects in the bombing. The prosecutor's office dropped the charges two months later for lack of evidence. Bari and Cherney then sued the FBI for placing the bomb, ultimately winning a $4.4 million settlement in 2002, although Bari had died of cancer in 1997.

Bari's skill for building coalition extended to other elements of Earth First! activism. Although aspects of the environmental movement have exhibited racist Malthusian and anti-immigrant politics, the deep ecology framework has also enabled inroads with land-based struggles of Indigenous sovereignty. In Minnesota, for instance, radical environmentalists teamed up with the Mendota Mdewakanton Dakota tribe to block road construction through a park the Dakotas held sacred. Together, the radicals built the "Minnehaha

Free State," a four-month-long land occupation in 1998. Destroying the free state was the largest police action in Minnesota history, involving eight hundred police officers evicting several dozen activists from six squatted homes. These and similar actions have often ended in jail time for participants—though, as with other nonviolent actions, the charges tend to be lower and the sentences shorter.

Starting in the mid-1990s, autonomous groups and individuals operating under the banner of the Earth Liberation Front (ELF) began carrying out more and more militant, clandestine acts of sabotage against a variety of targets—universities, corporations, real estate developments—accused of endangering the planet through genetic engineering, over-development, pollution, and conspicuous consumption. ELF actions (and those of the related Animal Liberation Front, ALF) have caused millions of dollars in damages in more than a thousand acts of arson across the country. As a result, the state has clamped down on the earth and animal liberation movements.

Particularly since 9/11, public animal rights and eco-activists have been called in front of grand juries, especially along the West Coast but also in the Midwest, and more than two dozen people have been arrested for suspected ALF or ELF activities. These cases have relied largely on the work of informants or infiltrators, and have produced some shockingly long sentences. Eric McDavid was sentenced to twenty years for a plan—never carried out and developed by a paid FBI infiltrator—to destroy cell phone towers. In another case, Marie Mason was sentenced to twenty-two years after admitting her involvement two ELF-motivated acts of property destruction after her ex-husband testified against her. She pleaded guilty to avoid a life sentence.

The most chilling aspect of these "Green Scare" arrests occurred as part of the FBI's called Operation Backfire. A case involving conspiracy and multiple arsons over a five-year period, Operation Backfire was frightening not just because it swept up more than a dozen people in its dragnet, but because the case was built almost entirely on informants.

Through threatening life in prison, the government successfully pressured eight defendants to cooperate (people who
themselves were arrested based on the extensive testimony
of one person, an alleged member of several ELF cells). And
yet, because the collaborators were often the most involved
in illegal activity, most of them ended up with longer sentences than those who maintained their principles.

The most public of the defendants who both refused to
cooperate with the government
investigation and connected
his case to other examples of
government repression was
Daniel McGowan. Arrested as
part of a coordinated national
sweep in 2005, McGowan was
sentenced to seven years in
prison (which included additional time added on as part
of a "terrorism enhancement"
sentencing structure). He spent
most of the last two years of his
sentence in a "Communications

Management Unit," a new structure of federal prisons where
prisoners are kept separate from the general population and
have extreme restrictions placed on their ability to commu-
nicate with people outside of prison. Authorities determine
at will who gets placed in a CMU; it is not connected to any
disciplinary infractions. McGowan and Andy Stephanian,
an animal rights activist also incarcerated in a CMU, both
reported that they were among the only non-Muslims held
in a CMU. The CMU is an expression of the security state at
its height, devising newer and crueler ways to isolate those
whose politics and worldview the state wishes to disappear.
McGowan joined a class-action suit against the government
in the hopes of exposing and shutting down the CMUs.
McGowan was released in December 2012. The lawsuit is
ongoing, with the CMUs still operational.

# Deja Vu and the Patriot Act

THE EARLY TWENTY-FIRST CENTURY HAS WITNESSED A CERTAIN DÉJÀ VU IN POLITICAL trials. Emboldened by the broad powers enabled through "fighting terrorism," the state has not only targeted a new crop of dissidents; it has arrested some old ones as well.

Perhaps most notorious is the case of eight former Black Panthers who were arrested on January 23, 2007, for the 1971 shooting death of a San Francisco police officer. Several of the men had already been arrested in New Orleans in the 1970s, and a judge had dismissed the charges when he found that their basis lay in confessions garnered through torture. In the post-9/11 environment, however, the San Francisco agents who oversaw the original investigation and torture came out of retirement to reprosecute the case. Five men were called in front of grand juries in 2005 and then thrown in jail when they refused to cooperate. The grand jury ultimately faded away, and the men were released, only to be arrested with others a year later in a case that had no known new evidence and ultimately cost millions of dollars without going to trial. (One of the five grand jury resisters, John Bowman, died of cancer shortly before the other eight were arrested.)

The eight were Herman Bell, Ray Boudreaux, Richard Brown, Hank Jones, Jalil Muntaqim, Richard O'Neal, Harold Taylor, and Francisco Torres. Bell and Muntaqim had already been in prison since 1971, being the two surviving members of the New York 3 who were framed for the murder of a New York City police officer that year. The state initially charged the men not only with the murder but with participating in a hazy conspiracy of Black militancy between 1968 and 1973. Ultimately, the state ended up dropping all charges against six of the eight, after Bell and Muntaqim pleaded guilty to lesser charges in order to return to New York State and continue their fight for parole.

In other revived cases, former BLA soldier Kamau Sadiki was sentenced to life in prison in 2003 for the 1971 death of a police officer in Georgia. Sadiki was arrested in New York in early 2001 on separate, but contemporary, charges that were subsequently dismissed. Once in custody, though, police officers tried to get his help in solving other BLA-suspected cases. That proved futile, but FBI files listed him as a suspect in the Atlanta killing and he was transferred to Georgia. The timing was a bit odd: the district attorney refused to prosecute the case in 1972 for insufficient evidence, there was no new evidence, and Sadiki had been living a quiet but nonetheless public life working for the phone company in New York City.

*Kamau Sadiki*

The Jericho Movement

Besides the Panthers, the other organization to be most subject to the politics of retrospective justice is the Symbionese Liberation Army (SLA). Perhaps the most controversial armed struggle organization of the 1970s, the SLA was a mostly white group based in California and formed under the leadership of a Black former prisoner who took the name Cinque, after the leader of a nineteenth-century slave rebellion. Several members of the group were lesbians; "symbionese" came from the word "symbiosis," as the group believed it was bringing together diverse elements of revolutionary thought. The group is best remembered for two actions: the murder of Oakland's superintendent of schools and the kidnapping of newspaper heiress Patty Hearst. The SLA assassinated Marc Foster, a well-liked Black administrator, for proposing a controversial student ID system. The group then kidnapped Patty Hearst, using her as ransom to force her wealthy family to provide food to Oakland's poor and to get their statements publicized. In an unexpected twist, Hearst later joined the group and participated in bank robberies to fund the group's activities, including one robbery gone awry, where a bystander was killed.

Five hundred Los Angeles police, FBI, and U.S. Treasury agents surrounded a house in Compton on May 17, 1974, where SLA members had been staying. Police fired tear gas and nine thousand bullets into the house, ultimately using an incendiary device to kill the six SLA members inside. Those remaining, and those who joined after the "Compton massacre," fled Los Angeles and eluded capture at least for another year. After Patty Hearst was arrested in 1975, she disassociated herself from the SLA and claimed her participation was a result of brainwashing. She was convicted, though President Carter commuted her sentence. Other members of the group also served several years in prison throughout the 1970s and 1980s.

In recent years, however, five former members of the group have found themselves in court for charges emanating from their activities in the 1970s. The SLA arrests include the extradition of James Kilgore from South Africa, where he had been living and working as a well-respected academic for years, and the arrest and trial of Kathy Soliah, who had been living a quiet life as Sara Jane Olson in Minnesota. Kilgore received a six-year sentence. Arrested shortly before 9/11, Soliah initially planned to fight her charges, but pleaded after the crumbling World Trade Center towers dashed her hopes of a fair trial. Sentenced to fourteen years, Olson was released on March 17, 2008, and rearrested a day later to serve another year of her sentence.

Emily Montague, Bill Harris, and Michael Bortin were also arrested and charged for their involvement in the SLA three decades earlier; they pleaded guilty in 2002 and were sentenced to eight, seven, and six years, respectively, for the accidental death of Myrna Opsahl in the failed bank robbery.

Three other post-9/11 prosecutions of 1960s-era radicals bear mentioning: H. Rap Brown, who famously declared violence to be "as American as cherry pie," was sentenced to life in prison in 2002 for the shooting death of a Fulton County sheriff's deputy two years earlier. The former leader of the Student Nonviolent Coordinating Committee had become imam of a Muslim community in Atlanta, changing his name to Jamil Al-Amin. As with Sadiki, Al-Amin denied any involvement in the shooting for which he was charged. He and his supporters allege the case to be the culmination of decades of harassment made possible by post-9/11 legal shifts. In two cases involving less famous activists, Canadian police arrested Gary Freeman (born Joseph Pannell) in 2004, and José Luis Jorge dos Santos (formerly George Wright) was arrested in Portugal in 2011. Both were accused of being former Black Panthers; Freeman was charged with having shot a Chicago police officer. Dos Santos, who had been incarcerated as a youth, hijacked a plane from Miami in 1972. Freeman pleaded guilty under an agreement that saw him serve just thirty days and pay restitution to a scholarship fund for the children of slain police officers. Though his case is more precarious, Portuguese authorities have refused to extradite Dos Santos.

The United States government's ongoing vendetta against political activists from a half-century ago can seem harsh and even irrational. Vengeful as it is, such prosecutions can also be understood as part of a coherent strategy of containment and dissuasion, the primary targets of which may not even have been born at the time of COINTELPRO, and may entertain political reference points generations removed from those of most of the prisoners discussed above. Many of these vindictive prosecutions decades after the fact took place in the decade after the anti-WTO actions at Seattle in 1999 and the Al Qaeda attacks on September 11, 2001. More recently, in the years following the 2008 financial crisis, governments around the world have been faced with an abrupt upsurge in protests of various forms—from Arab Spring to Occupy Wall Street and Idle No More, among others—involving both longtime activists and hundreds of thousands of people who may never have been involved in protest movements before. This upsurge has manifested itself in different forms reflecting different politics, and adopting different tactics and strategies.

In this context, those adopting more confrontational tactics have found themselves the targets of much the same kinds of state repression as the radicals of movements past. Thus, this carceral déjà vu is not just an issue of old cases from the 1970s. It is also a matter of expanding repression in the twenty-first century. A few cases stand out here. Longtime activist and radical attorney Lynne Stewart—who has represented David Gilbert, Bilal Sunni-Ali, and Richard Williams among others—was one of the first domestic targets of the post-9/11 War on Terror. Adding to the bizarre circumstances of her case, Attorney General John Ashcroft first announced charges against her on a late-night television talk show in 2002. She was charged with conspiracy and providing material support to terrorists after delivering a public message on behalf of her client, Egyptian cleric Omar Abdel-Rahman, who was being held in isolation at a supermax prison for his role in the 1994 World Trade Center bombing. Sentenced to twenty-eight months in prison in 2006, the state appealed Stewart's sentence and in 2009, at the age of seventy, Stewart was resentenced to ten years. A court upheld her sentence in 2012. Amid her incarceration, however, Stewart was battling stage-four breast cancer. Supporters pressured the Justice Department for compassionate release for more than a year, which was finally granted on the last day of 2013.

Stewart's case was among the most publicized in a slew of post-9/11 conspiracy charges prosecuted under the mantle of counterterrorism. Conspiracy is a vague legal category that does not require the accused to have participated in illegal activity to be guilty of allegedly dangerous associations. Its capaciousness has proven a convenient way to target different anarchist networks and radical groups who have planned protests, participated in direct actions, or organized international solidarity efforts.

A quick overview of such repression during the Obama era includes a string of cases around the country: eight Minneapolis anarchists were charged with conspiracy for organizing public protests against the 2008 Republican National Convention in Minnesota (in 2010, five defendants pleaded guilty in exchange for probation, community service or, for one, a short jail sentence; charges were dropped against the other three); a series of police raids and grand jury investigations between 2010 and 2013 against anarchists in Portland, Olympia, and Seattle as well as against members of the communist Freedom Road Socialist Organization in Chicago, Los Angeles, and Minneapolis resulted in a series of people spending weeks or months in jail for refusing to cooperate with grand juries (all of the cases are ongoing); and several young activists, some of them connected to different sections of the Occupy movement, have been entrapped by police agents. These entrapments range from two young anarchists set up by FBI informant Brandon Darby during the 2008 RNC protests in St. Paul to several young men arrested in 2012 on different bomb plots. Five men were arrested in Cleveland, Ohio, in May for plotting to blow up a bridge; shortly thereafter three Occupy activists were arrested with Molotov cocktails during protests against a NATO meeting in Chicago. In Chicago, Cleveland, and St. Paul, police informants had encouraged or designed the plans; in some cases they acquired the bomb-making materials themselves. (The RNC protestors were sentenced to twenty-four months; the Cleveland five were sentenced to serve six to ten years or more in prison; the NATO 3 case is ongoing as of 2013.)

There is another invidious element to this post-9/11 déjà vu, and that is the way in which the American government has revived a slew of COINTELPRO-esque dirty tricks in the context of the PATRIOT ACT in order to prosecute Arab and Muslim men inside the United States. In a variety of cases across the country, the government has used informants, entrapment, surveillance, and Islamophobia to indict, arrest, and imprison a variety of Arab and Muslim people, mostly men. These cases have tended to proceed along one of two fronts: either undercover operatives have worked to entrap Muslim men in a bomb plot cooked up by the agent (as in the Newburgh 4 case, among many others), or the state charges people with conspiracy and terrorism charges based on their financial or vocal support for different organizations or campaigns in the Middle East, often involving Palestine— as happened to Sami Al-Arian, the Holy Land 7, and Tarek Mehanna, among others. These trials utilize the social and familial networks alongside the travel patterns of the accused in order to identify as agents of international terrorism people who are critical of U.S. foreign policy. While some of these defendants do not have progressive or radical politics (or even, necessarily, a developed sense of politics), these cases have not involved al-Qaeda members or people with any kind of military directives or training. Taking place alongside the torture and indefinite detention of Guantánamo Bay, Abu Ghraib, Bagram Air Force Base and a variety of "black sites" scattered throughout the world, these cases demonstrate that the War on Terror has needed imprisonment—at home and abroad. The prison and the particular set of policies and ideologies that sustain it are essential ingredients for how the United States addresses race, region, religion, and radicalism.

# Conclusion: A New Beginning

WHILE THE UNITED STATES DENIES THE EXISTENCE OF POLITI-CAL PRISONERS, IT PURSUES a vengeful policy of lengthy, even lifelong, incarceration. To acknowledge the political basis of their incarceration would further expose the depths of social problems that these militants have committed their lives to fighting. The veneer of U.S. democracy and tolerance requires that dissidents be branded as criminals, or terrorists, and denial of the humanity of anyone so labeled. Working to free political prisoners goes hand in hand with exposing the façade that the United States is a country where injustice is minimal and solved through electoral politics—one point necessitates the other. The fact that so many political prisoners have been charged with treason or sedition demonstrates that the government fears this precise point; resistance is criminalized, deemed a threat to "the American way of life." The ubiquity of state repression affords an opportunity to forge solidarity among multiple revolutionary movements. Seizing this opportunity does not mean ignoring contradictions (e.g., the difference between pacifism and armed struggle, anarchism and Marxism-Leninism, secularism and faith-based organizing, or the struggles within particular movements over racism and patriarchy). Instead, it offers a chance for people committed to radical social change to work with one another, addressing differences in ways that build alliances and strengthen the potential for revolutionary possibilities. The fact that most political prisoners have continued their political work in prison—through writing, mentoring younger activists, conducting peer education with other prisoners, and fighting AIDS, misogyny, and homophobia—provides a worthy example to follow.

Most governments routinely release political prisoners every decade or so, and political internees are often incarcerated together or allowed increased family visits, in tacit recognition of the political nature of their "crimes." Not so in the

United States, where "amnesty" is a forbidden term. The FBI, Police Benevolent Associations, U.S. Parole Commission, and similar entities have routinely lobbied hard to prevent parole, even when people meet all standards for release (e.g., good records, jobs available upon release, community support). In perhaps the most frightening example, former Panther Veronza Bowers has been kept in prison more than eight years past his mandatory release date, without cause or indication of when he will get out. The government has regularly pointed to the "serious charges" and prior political affiliations of the prisoners as reasons for their ongoing incarceration—even though parole is supposed to evaluate someone's time in prison as a metric for their possible release rather than the charges that resulted in their imprisonment, since the charges never change.

Further, the recent popular attention given to "mass incarceration" in the United States, alongside public hand-wringing over the tremendous cost of such widespread confinement, creates the possibility for generating broad-based movements dedicated to shrinking the carceral state as such. This is a new and exciting development. The issue of incarceration itself—including not just political prisoners but the prison as a system—needs to be framed as a fundamental question of building and defending our movements. This is a movement rooted in care: It means supporting prisoners as part of a movement culture where people care for one another, create new bonds of solidarity, and celebrate people's history. This is a movement focused on shrinking the state's capacity to repress: It means working to close prisons, end solitary confinement, free prisoners, eliminate borders. It means embedding direct challenges to the carceral state within social struggles while working to popularize a wider set of radical politics. While no one organization can do

Dave Onion / multi.lectical.net

everything, a successful anti-prison movement will need to synthesize direct action, popular relevancy, and radical critique. To separate these approaches is to grant victory to the prison state.

The prison can be seen as an extension of the repression that drove many of these people to undertake militant action in the first place. It is part of the government's arsenal to destroy revolutionaries. The state has sometimes made this explicit by housing radicals in control unit prisons, prisons-within-prisons that are based on solitary confinement and sensory deprivation. The prisons in Florence, Colorado, and Marion, Illinois, are the best examples of this, and those institutions have housed Ray Luc Levasseur, Mutulu Shakur, Bill Dunne, and Yu Kikumura, among others. The most famous example of a political prison was the Lexington Control Unit, a basement prison in Kentucky that held former May 19th activists Silvia Baraldini and Susan Rosenberg and Puerto Rican independentista Alejandrina Torres from 1986 to 1988. The prison was so oriented toward inducing physical and psychological ailments that Amnesty International declared it cruel and unusual punishment; a grassroots campaign succeeded in closing the unit, but supermax prisons remain, and have indeed metastasized across penal America, currently holding an unknown number of prisoners suspected of political activities or opinions hostile to the governing order.

The bulk of such repression is meted out against revolutionary people of color, particularly Black, Native American, and Puerto Rican radicals. The reasons for this are complex—they involve not just white privilege but the fact that the government has taken a firm position against the release of any political prisoner with a murder conviction. Due to the open levels of confrontation between police and communities of color, these liberation movements often adopted different tactics than white militants. But the state's intransigence on paroling those with murder convictions has repercussions for political prisoners regardless of race—several white anti-imperialists are also imprisoned for the deaths of law enforcement agents, seemingly with no chance of release.

The political incarceration of people who became active in the 1960s is inextricably tied to state repression. Even when they committed illegal acts or acts of which they themselves are now critical, their continuing incarceration cannot be separated from the legacy of COINTELPRO. Even now, movement veterans captured as a result of movement work in the 1960s are paying for the state's crimes through continued incarceration. The ongoing imprisonment of '60s-era activists—together with a new breed of political prisoners coming from an array of contemporary movements, as well as the politicized prisoners organizing in prisons around the country—presents a direct connection between the struggles of yesterday and those of today.

There are serious challenges to this work, including limited resources, a strategy that must deal with the legal system, public fear of "terrorists," and the difficulty of building working relationships among the various movements and communities who find themselves experiencing state repression. But combating political incarceration and supporting those in the crosshairs of state repression remain central to creating a better future. After all, the government remembers who joins and organizes in the movement, regardless of whether they do so before, during, or after their time in prison. Social movements cannot afford to forget.

Bill Hackwell

# Afterword
*dream hampton*

Our lives and our movements today are as—maybe unknowingly—shaped by the political prisoners who still sit behind concrete walls as the prisons themselves invisibly shape the landscape of the world we seek to make more just. It's no coincidence that many of my greatest heroes had their lives either ended by the state or have been tried, convicted, and jailed for nothing more than the "crime" of loving their people enough to attempt a revolution in the United States.

If prisons are an "index of injustice," as Berger says, then our resistance to them and connection to those inside can be a measure of our movements as well.

As time marches on from the height of liberation struggles that produced many of the political prisoners, our prisoners, our work is not just to see them freed but also to ensure they and their work is remembered and kept current. Berger's book is a key weapon in the war against forgetting, arming us with the most dangerous ammunition there is; a collective memory and connected link in our long chain of struggle.

For ten years I helped coordinate the New York chapter celebration of Black August, a tradition that began in San Quentin Prison after the assassination of revolutionary human and prisoners' rights activist and author George Jackson in 1971 and the murder of another San Quentin inmate, Khatari Gaulden, eight years later, who had carried on Jackson's work after his death. Jackson's death, for which the prison absolved itself and the guards responsible, sparked the famous rebellion in Attica and informed the uprisings of prisoners across the country. Gaulden's 1979 murder formalized the tradition of Black August as a time of fasting, studying, and exercising to commemorate their deaths and carry on their legacy. To this day, Black August is a tradition that unites prisoners and those on the outside who support them and join them in sun up to sun down fasting, studying of radical reading materials, remembering histories of Black liberation, and improving ourselves through exercise. It is a tradition of traditions, a tradition of struggle, love, and community.

Fifteen years after its start, Black August took on new dimensions in 1994 when Ahmed Obafemi, of the New Afrikan's Peoples Organization approached what was then a brand new chapter of Malcolm X Grassroots Organization about focusing the month to use hip hop to raise money and awareness for and about U.S. political prisoners. Obafemi's ask was an extension of one made by Assata Shakur to the attendees of Havana's World Youth Day two years earlier: how to use the latest promise of Black culture in service of our revolutionary movements?

Assata is a hero to so many of us and to me personally. Her self-titled autobiography changed my life. Hers is a clear, sober reflection of the Black Panther Party she joined when she was a student organizer in New York's City College in Harlem. Assata's analysis of the intersection of race and capitalism in the United States is fortified by the revolutionary work she did as a community organizer. She was as fearless confronting drug dealers whose shooting resulted in the death of a neighborhood child as she was confronting police brutality and harassment and political oppression. That she now lives in Cuba, a free but hunted woman, after being framed and unjustly convicted by what she rightly described as a "kangaroo court," only makes her journey more epic and triumphant.

But when those of us in awe of Assata were actually able to talk to her, it changed the conversation. She was not just a symbol but a living, breathing person with whom we could exchange ideas, strategy, laughter. She was, and is, our comrade—she is not, and never was or will be, the million-dollar bounty that the state of New Jersey has put on her head. Her significance is not the fact that she was, in 2012, the first woman placed on the same Most Wanted FBI terrorist list that once included Osama bin Laden. It is her still tireless determination and clarity about the need to fight for others. When

Assata is able to meet with activists from the United States she insists that they direct the energy that would be spent defending her to the defense campaign of her codefendant Sundiata Acoli. Like Assata, Acoli was injured and arrested by the New Jersey State police, an encounter that left Zayd Shakur and a New Jersey trooper dead. Unlike Assata, Acoli is still serving time in prison. Indeed, he has been locked up consistently since 1973, bounced around between a series of federal prisons around the country even though his charges originate in New Jersey.

Enter the importance of *The Struggle Within*. Sundiata Acoli is one of sixty-five political prisoners listed on The Jericho Movement's website. Most of these prisoners have been in prison my entire life. Through J. Edgar Hoover's COINTELPRO they were framed, hunted, and convicted in complicated ways. Various police agencies created the conditions for such long-term imprisonment of our comrades, regardless of whether they were framed whole cloth or prosecuted for actions they undertook against state violence. The accusations brought against them included charges of murder, and sometimes, as with Assata Shakur, Sundiata Acoli, Leonard Peltier, and several others who have served decades in prison, with the murder of a police officer.

There are shining moments and exceptions among the outrage that is the story of political prisoners in the United States. Geronimo Pratt was a Panther who saw his conviction overturned after twenty-seven years, work that the legendary attorney Johnnie Cochran considered the most important of his storied career. Dhoruba bin Wahad was another Black Panther able to overturn his conviction after nineteen years locked up. The Puerto Rican independence movement has freed several generations of its political prisoners, women and men serving what would otherwise have been functionally life sentences.

Yet dozens more remain behind walls, often isolated, and at times tortured for their political beliefs. To accept this fact is to ask what ideas can be so dangerous that those who hold it in their heads must be hidden from us? To understand that these people and their circumstance do indeed exist, is a necessary first step for a country whose cloak of democracy keeps us in denial. Americans believe political prisoners are a fact in countries like China, Iran, and Cuba but live the lie of the U.S. government's denial of the existence of U.S. political prisoners in its borders.

*The Struggle Within* and the decades of radical movements it chronicles shatter that lie. This book puts us back in proximity to the people and the movements that prisons are meant to place out of reach. To be reconnected to them is to be committed to their freedom. Not solely because they deserve to be free or because our communities would be that much stronger if we had them home, but because for activists today to have the confidence to take the risks and make the leaps that these times require, we must know that we will catch each other when we fall or care for each other if and when and the state seeks to treat us in the same way as those who came before us.

By refusing to allow targeted leaders to be taken from us, we take away the state's strongest threat. To fight for the freedom of political prisoners is to declare that there is no barbed wire sharp enough to keep us apart. It includes the cell block in our strategy, and it affirms what Assata taught us and continues to teach us: that a wall is just a wall, and nothing more at all. It can be broken down.

Free All Political Prisoners.

# A Bibliographic Note

While I have not included footnotes for reasons of space, this book was written in consultation with a vast array of archives and sources—including a wide variety of interviews, essays, pamphlets, books, and videos. Below I provide a list of some of the key texts useful in thinking about prisons, political prisoners, and mass movements in the United States. The list is, at best, woefully incomplete and focused on books rather than the countless good articles, essays, pamphlets, and documentaries about these subjects. Still, the following bibliography should provide a good start to those curious for more reading. Fortunately, with more and more people studying these issues, the next few years should leave us with a better record. The list below is meant to supplement rather than replace direct contact with prisoners, former prisoners, and organizers working for a world without cages. It is up to date as of January 2014.

## PRISON ORGANIZING

Dan Berger, *Captive Nation: Black Prison Organizing in the Civil Rights Era* (UNC Press, 2014)

Tim Blunk and Ray Luc Levasseur (eds.), *Hauling Up the Morning: Writings and Art by Political Prisoners and Prisoners of War in the U.S.* (The Red Sea Press, 1990)

Committee to End the Marion Lockdown, *Can't Jail the Spirit: Biographies of U.S. Political Prisoners* (2002 or other editions)

Critical Resistance Publications Collective, *Abolition Now!* (AK Press, 2008)

Alan Eladio Gomez, "Resisting Living Death at Marion Federal Penitentiary, 1972," *Radical History Review* 96, 58-86

Rebecca Hill, *Men, Mobs, and Law: Antilynching and Labor Defense in U.S. Radical History* (Duke University Press, 2007)

Joy James, ed., *The Angela Y. Davis Reader* (Blackwell Publishers, 1998)

Joy James, ed., *Imprisoned Intellectuals: America's Political Prisoners Write on Life, Liberation and Rebellions* (Rowman and Littlefield, 2003)

Nancy Kurshan, *Out of Control* (Freedom Archives, 2013)

Victoria Law, *Resistance Behind Bars: The Struggles of Incarcerated Women* (PM Press, 2012)

Matt Meyer, ed., *Let Freedom Ring: Documents from the Movements to Free U.S. Political Prisoners* (PM Press, 2008)

Christian Parenti, *Lockdown America: Police and Prisons in an Age of Crisis* (Verso, 2000)

Resistance in Brooklyn, *Enemies of the State* (Kersplebedeb, 1998)

Beth Ritchie, *Arrested Justice: Black Women, Violence, and America's Prison Nation* (NYU Press, 2012)

Elihu Rosenblatt, ed., *Criminal Injustice: Confronting the Prison Crisis* (South End Press, 1996).

## POLICING AND PRISONS

Trevor Aaronson, *The Terror Factory: Inside the FBI's Manufactured War on Terror* (Ig Publishing, 2013)

Michelle Alexander, *The New Jim Crow: Mass Incarceration in an Age of Colorblindness* (New Press, 2010)

Ward Churchill and Jim Vander Wall, *Agents of Repression: The FBI's Secret Wars Against the Black Panther Party and the American Indian Movement* (South End Press, 1988) and *The COINTELPRO Papers: Documents from the FBI's Secret War Against Dissent in the United States* (South End Press, 1990)

David Cunningham, *There's Something Happening Here: The New Left, the Klan and FBI Counterintelligence* (University of California Press, 2005)

Frank Donner, *Protectors of Privilege: Red Squads and Police Repression in Urban America* (University of California Press, 1992) and *The Age of Surveillance* (Vintage, 1981)

Pascal Emmer, Adrian Lowe, and R. Barrett Marshall, *This Is a Prison: Glitter Is Not Allowed* (Hearts on a Wire, 2011)

Luis Fernandez, *Policing Dissent: Social Control and the Anti-globalization Movement* (Rutgers University Press, 2008)

Ruth Wilson Gilmore, *Golden Gulag: Prisons, Surplus, Crisis, and Opposition in Globalizing California* (University of California Press, 2007)

Marie Gottschalk, *The Prison and the Gallows: The Politics of Mass Incarceration in America* (Oxford University Press, 2006)

Joy James, ed., *States of Confinement: Policing, Detention, and Prisons* (Palgrave McMillan, 2002) and *Warfare in the American Homeland* (Duke University Press, 2007)

Laleh Khalili, *Time in the Shadows: Confinement in Counterinsurgencies* (Stanford University Press, 2012)

Regina Kunzel, *Criminal Intimacy: Prison and the Uneven History of Modern American Sexuality* (Chicago University Press, 2008)

Ken Lawrence, *The New State Repression* (Tarantula Pamphlets, 2006)

Jenna Loyd, Matt Mitchelson, and Andrew Burridge, eds., *Beyond Walls and Cages: Prisons, Borders, and Global Crisis* (University of Georgia Press, 2012)

Tram Nguyn, *We Are All Suspects Now* (Beacon, 2005)

Kenneth O'Reilly, *Racial Matters: The FBI's Secret File on Black America, 1960–1972* (Free Press, 1991)

Robert Perkinson, *Texas Tough: The Rise of America's Prison Empire* (Metropolitan Books, 2010)

Bud and Ruth Schultz, *It Did Happen Here: Recollections of Political Repression in America* (University of California Press, 1989)

Eric Stanley and Nat Smith, *Captive Genders: Trans Embodiment and the Prison Industrial Complex* (AK Press, 2011)

Heather Ann Thompson, "Why Mass Incarceration Matters," *Journal of American History* vol. 97, no. 3, 703–34

Kristian Williams, William Munger, and Lara Messersmith-Glavin, *Life During Wartime: Resisting Counterinsurgency* (AK Press, 2013).

# NORTH AMERICAN FREEDOM MOVEMENTS

Mumia Abu-Jamal, *We Want Freedom: A Life in the Black Panther Party* (South End Press, 2006)

Kuwasi Balagoon, *A Soldier's Story* (Kersplebedeb, 2003)

Terry Bisson, *On a MOVE: The Story of Mumia Abu-Jamal* (Litmus Books, 2000)

Patricia Bell Blawis, *Tijerina and the Land Grants: Mexican Americans in Struggle for Their Heritage* (International Publishers, 1971)

Joshua Bloom and Waldo Martin, *Black Against Empire: The History of the Black Panther Party* (University of California Press, 2013)

Safiya Bukhari, *The War Before* (The Feminist Press, 2010)

Kathleen Cleaver and George Katsiaficas, eds., *Liberation, Imagination, and the Black Panther Party* (Routledge, 2001)

Charles Jones, ed., *The Black Panther Party Reconsidered* (Black Classics Press, 1998)

Peter Matthiessen, *In the Spirit of Crazy Horse* (New York: Penguin, 1991)

MOVE, *Twenty-Five Years on the MOVE* (self-published)

Donna Murch, *Living for the City: Education, Migration, and the Rise of the Black Panther Party* (UNC Press, 2010)

Lorena Oropeza, *Raza Si! Guerra No! Chicano Protest and Patriotism During the Viet Nam War Era* (University of California Press, 2005)

Vijay Prashad, *The Darker Nations: A People's History of the Third World* (New Press, 2007)

Laura Pulido, *Black, Brown, Yellow & Left: Radical Activism in Los Angeles* (University of California Press, 2006)

J. Sakai, *Settlers: The Mythology of the White Proletariat* (Chicago: Morningstar, 1989)

E. Tani and Kae Sera, *False Nationalism, False
Internationalism: Class Contradictions in the Armed Struggle*
(Seeds Beneath the Snow, 1985)
Andrés Torres and José E. Velázquez, eds., *The Puerto Rican
Movement: Voices from the Diaspora* (Temple University
Press, 1998)
Akinyele Umoja, *We Will Shoot Back: Armed Resistance in the
Mississippi Freedom Movement* (NYU Press, 2013)
Ernesto B. Vigil, *The Crusade for Justice: Chicano Militancy
and the Government's War on Dissent* (University of
Wisconsin Press, 1999)
Cynthia Young, *Soul Power: Culture, Radicalism, and the Making
of a U.S. Third World Left* (Duke University Press, 2006)

# ANTI-AUTHORITARIANISM
# AND ANTI-IMPERIALISM

Bill Ayers, Bernardine Dohrn, and Jeff Jones, eds., *Sing a
Battle Song: The Revolutionary Poetry, Statements, and
Communiques of the Weather Underground 1970–1974*
(Seven Stories Press, 2007)
Dan Berger, *Outlaws of America: The Weather Underground
and the Politics of Solidarity* (AK Press, 2006)
Daniel Burton-Rose, *Guerrilla USA: The George Jackson
Brigade and the Anti-capitalist Underground of the 1970s*
(University of California Press, 2010)
Daniel Burton-Rose, ed., *Creating a Movement with Teeth: A
Documentary History of the George Jackson Brigade* (PM
Press, 2010)
Daniel S. Chard, "Rallying for Repression: Police Terror, Law
and Order Politics, and the Decline of Maine's Prisoners'
Rights Movement," in *The Sixties* vol. 5, no. 1, 47–73
Ward Churchill with Mike Ryan, *Pacifism as Pathology:
Reflections on the Role of Armed Struggle in North America*
(AK Press, 2007)

Roxanne Dunbar-Ortiz, *Outlaw Woman: A Memoir of the War Years, 1960–1975* (City Lights, 2004)

George Katsiaficas, *The Imagination of the New Left* (South End Press, 1987)

The New Yippie Book Collective, *Blacklisted News, Secret Histories: From Chicago to 1984* (Berkeley: Bleecker Publishing, 1983)

Becky Thompson, *A Promise and a Way of Life: White Antiracist Activism* (University of Minnesota Press, 2000)

Jeremy Varon, *Bringing the War Home: The Weather Underground, the Red Army Faction, and Revolutionary Violence in the Sixties and Seventies* (University of California Press, 2004).


# REVOLUTIONARY NONVIOLENCE


Scott H. Bennett, *Radical Pacifism: The War Resisters League and Gandhian Nonviolence in America, 1915–1963* (Syracuse University Press, 2003)

Daniel Berrigan, *The Trial of the Catonsville 9* (Fordham University Press, 2004)

Andrew Cornell, *Oppose and Propose: Lessons from the Movement for a New Society* (AK Press, 2011)

Dave Dellinger, *More Power Than We Know: The People's Movement for Democracy* (Anchor Press, 1975)

Barbara Deming, *Remembering Who We Are* (Pagoda, 1981)

Barbara Epstein, *Political Protest and Cultural Revolution: Nonviolent Direct Action in the 1970s and 1980s* (University of California Press, 1991)

Joseph Kip Kosek, *Acts of Conscience: Christian Nonviolence and Modern American Democracy* (Columbia University Press, 2009)

Arthur J. Laffin and Anne Montgomery, eds., *Swords into Plowshares: Nonviolent Direct Action for Disarmament* (Harper & Row, 1987)

Staughton and Alice Lynd, *Nonviolence in America: A Documentary History* (Orbis, 1995)

Elizabeth 'Betita' Martínez, Matt Meyer, and Mandy Carter, *We Have Not Been Moved: Resisting Racism and Militarism in 21st Century America* (PM Press, 2012) Pam McAllister, ed., *Reweaving the Web of Life: Feminism and Nonviolence* (New Society Publishers, 1982)

Pam McAllister, *You Can't Kill the Spirit: Stories of Women and Nonviolent Action* (New Society Publishers, 1988)

Jane Meyerding, ed., *We Are All Part of One Another: A Barbara Deming Reader* (New Society Publishers, 1984)

Murray Polner, *Disarmed and Dangerous: The Radical Life and Times of Daniel and Philip Berrigan* (Westview Press, 1997)

James Tracy, *Direct Action: Radical Pacifism from the Union Eight to the Chicago Seven* (University of Chicago Press, 1996).

# EARTH AND ANIMAL LIBERATION

Steve Best and Anthony Nocella, *Igniting a Revolution: Voices in Defense of the Earth* (AK Press, 2006)

Direct Action Manual Collective, *Earth First! Direct Action Manual* (1997)

Dave Foreman, *Ecodefense: A Field Guide to Monkeywrenching* (Abbzug Press, 1997)

Derrick Jensen, *Endgame* [2 volumes] (Seven Stories Press, 2006)

Christopher Manes, *Green Rage: Radical Environmentalism and the Unmaking of Civilization* (Back Bay Books, 1991)

Leslie James Pickering, *Earth Liberation Front, 1997–2002* (Arissa Media Group, 2007)

Will Potter, *Green Is the New Red* (City Lights, 2011)

Craig Rosebraugh, *Burning Rage of a Dying Planet: Speaking for the Earth Liberation Front* (Lantern Books, 2004).

# Organizational Resources

Below is a list of some of the many organizations working to support political prisoners and end the carceral state. Many of the individuals mentioned in *The Struggle Within* have their own defense or support committees. For reasons of space, however, this list excludes individual support or defense committees (for links to those, see the Jericho Movement website). The following list provides only the national office or primary contact of organizations that have multiple chapters. Thanks to Bob Lederer and Sara Falconer for first compiling many of these addresses for the anthology *Let Freedom Ring*.

**All of Us or None**
c/o LSPC (see below)
415-255-7036 x 337
Linda@prisonerswithchildren.org
Manuel@prisonerswithchildren.org

Local chapters in Oakland, Sacramento, East Palo Alto, Los Angeles, Long Beach, San Bernadino, San Diego, Detroit, Oklahoma City, and San Antonio.

*All of Us or None is a grassroots civil rights organization fighting for the rights of formerly and currently incarcerated people and our families. We are fighting against the discrimination that people face every day because of arrest or conviction history. The goal of All of Us or None is to strengthen the voices of people most affected by mass incarceration and the growth of the prison-industrial complex. Through our grassroots organizing, we will build a powerful political movement to win full restoration of our human and civil rights.*

Dave Onion / multi.lectical.net

## Anarchist Black Cross Federation
www.abcf.net • info@abcf.net

*The ABCF works to support political prisoners through building alliances and raising funds. If emailing the address above, include "prisonspam" in the subject to avoid being caught by the spam filter. The ABCF has several chapters:*

**Los Angeles ABCF**
P.O. Box 11223
Whittier CA 90603
la@abcf.net

**Philadelphia ABCF**
P.O. Box 42129
Philadelphia, PA 19101
timABCF@aol.com

**New York City ABCF**
P.O. Box 110034
Brooklyn, New York 11211
nycabc@riseup.net

**South Brooklyn ABCF**
sbrooklynabcf@riseup.net

## Books Through Bars Philadelphia
4722 Baltimore Avenue, Philadelphia, PA 19143
215-727-8170
info@booksthroughbars.org • www.booksthroughbars.org

*Books Through Bars provides quality reading material to prisoners and encourage creative dialogue on the criminal justice system. BTB has created an interactive map showing prison book programs in the U.S. and Canada, including contact information. BTB also runs the Address This! Education Program that provides correspondence courses for Pennsylvania prisoners in solitary confinement.*

## Center for Constitutional Rights
666 Broadway, 7th Floor, New York, NY 10012
212-614-6464
www.ccrjustice.org

*The Center for Constitutional Rights is dedicated to advancing and protecting the rights guaranteed by the United States Constitution and the Universal Declaration of Human Rights.*

**Certain Days: Freedom for Political Prisoners Calendar**
c/o QPIRG Concordia, 1455 de Maisonneuve Boulevard O.,
Montreal, QC H3G 1M8, Canada
info@certaindays.org • www.certaindays.org

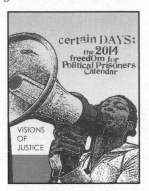

*The calendar is a joint fund-raising and educational project between outside organizers in Montreal and Toronto and three political prisoners held in maximum-security prisons in New York State: Herman Bell, David Gilbert, and Robert "Seth" Hayes. We work from an anti-imperialist, anti-racist, anti-capitalist, feminist, queer, and trans positive position, and the calendar serves as an annual benefit for various radical organizations around the world.*

**California Coalition for Women Prisoners**
1540 Market St., Suite 490, San Francisco, CA 94102
415-255-7036 x 4
info@womenprisoners.org • www.womenprisoners.org

*CCWP is a grassroots social justice organization, with members inside and outside prison, that challenges the institutional violence imposed on women, transgender people, and communities of color by the prison industrial complex (PIC). We see the struggle for racial and gender justice as central to dismantling the PIC and we prioritize the leadership of the people, families, and communities most impacted in building this movement.*

**California Prison Focus**
1904 Franklin St., Oakland, CA 94612
510-836-7222
contact@prisons.org • www.prisons.org

*California Prison Focus works with and on behalf of prisoners in California's state prisons, and publishes the Prison Focus newsletter available for free to SHU prisoners (and for a small donation to other prisoners).*

## Californians United for a Responsible Budget (CURB)

1322 Webster St. #210, Oakland, CA 94612-3217

info@curbprisonspending.org • www.curbprisonspending.org

*CURB is a broad-based coalition of over 40 organizations seeking to curb prison spending by reducing the number of people in prison and the number of prisons in the state.*

## Campaign to End the New Jim Crow

www.endnewjimcrow.org

*Campaign to End the New Jim Crow is a project of New York City's Riverside Church Prison Ministry working to end mass incarceration through public education, study groups, and campaigns against racist police practices such as stop-and-frisk.*

## Critical Resistance National Office

1904 Franklin St., Suite 504, Oakland, CA 94612

510-444-0484

crnational@criticalresistance.org • www.criticalresistance.org

Local chapters in Los Angeles, New Orleans, Oakland.

*Critical Resistance seeks to build an international movement to end the prison industrial complex by challenging the belief that caging and controlling people makes us safe. We believe that basic necessities such as food, shelter, and freedom are what really make our communities secure; as such, our work is part of global struggles against inequality and powerlessness.*

## Courage to Resist

484 Lake Park Avenue, #41, Oakland, CA 94610

510-488-3559

www.couragetoresist.org • www.facebook.com/couragetoresist

*Courage to Resist is a group of concerned community members, veterans, and military families that supports military objectors to illegal war and occupation and the policies of empire.*

**Decarcerate PA**
P.O. Box 40764, Philadelphia, PA 19107
267-217-3372
decarceratepa@gmail.com • www.decarceratepa.info

*Decarcerate PA is a grassroots campaign working to end mass incarceration in Pennsylvania. We demand that the state stop building prisons, reduce the prison population, and reinvest money in our communities.*

**Denver Anarchist Black Cross**
P.O. Box 11236, Denver, CO 80211
denverabc@riseup.net • denverabc.wordpress.com
facebook.com/denverabc

*Providing support to political prisoners, prisoners of war and social movements since 2009.*

**Detention Watch Network**
P.O. Box 43101, Washington, DC 20010
202-350-9055
sshah@detentionwatchnetwork.org
www.detentionwatchnetwork.org

*DWN is a national coalition of organizations and individuals working to expose and challenge the injustices of the U.S. immigration detention and deportation system and advocate for profound change that promotes the rights and dignity of all persons.*

**Dream Defenders**
www.dreamdefenders.org

Local chapters in Tallahassee, Gainesville, Orlando, Tampa, and Miami.

*Dream Defenders is a human rights organization, directed by Black and Brown youth who confront inequality and the criminalizing of our generation with nonviolent direct action and building of collective power in our communities.*

**The Florence Immigrant and Refugee Rights Project**
P.O. Box 654, Florence, AZ 85132
520-868-0191
firrp@firrp.org • www.firrp.org

*The Florence Project provides free legal services to men, women, and unaccompanied children detained by Immigration and Customs Enforcement (ICE) in Arizona.*


**4strugglemag: Views, Thoughts and Analysis from the Hearts and Minds of North American Political Prisoners and Friends**
P.O. Box 97048, RPO Roncesvalles Avenue, Toronto, ON
M6R 3B3 Canada
jaanlaaman@gmail.com
www.4strugglemag.org (all issues available online)

*This magazine, edited by Ohio 7 political prisoner Jaan Laaman and members of Toronto Anarchist Black Cross, focuses the insights and experiences of U.S. political prisoners on major issues of the day. Hard copies are available (free to prisoners, $5 an issue for people outside). We encourage readers to respond, critique, and carry on discussions in the magazine.*


**Freedom Archives**
522 Valencia St., San Francisco, CA 94110
415-863-9977
info@freedomarchives.org • www.freedomarchives.org

*Freedom Archives is a nonprofit educational media archive dedicated to the preservation and dissemination of historical audio and video documenting progressive movements from the 1960s to the present. The Archives offers a youth development program that encourages engagement with these historical materials and offers media production training. The Archives produces a variety of print, audio, and online media relating to prisons and political prisoners, among other topics. The Archives also edits an e-newsletter, "Political Prisoner News"—subscribe via the Freedom Archives website.*

**Grand Jury Resistance Project (GJRP)**
www.grandjuryresistance.org

*The GJRP is a coalition of lawyers, activists, and individuals targeted by government harassment working to coordinate powerful and effective resistance across the country to the epidemic of governmental political repression waged in the form of grand jury investigations, surveillance, political prosecutions, and collaboration between federal and local agencies to deny basic constitutional rights.*

**Guelph Anarchist Black Cross**
P.O. Box 183, Guelph, ON, Canada, N1H 6J6
guelphabc@riseup.net • guelphabc.noblogs.org

*The Guelph Anarchist Black Cross provides support to politicized prisoners with a focus on Southern Ontario (Canada).*

**Incite! Women of Color Against Violence**
P.O. Box 226, Redmond, WA 98073
484-932-3166 • www.incite-national.org

Local chapters in Ann Arbor, San Francisco Bay Area, Binghamton, Denver, Fort Collins, Los Angeles, New Orleans, New York, Washington, DC

*INCITE! Women of Color Against Violence is a national activist organization of radical feminists of color advancing a movement to end violence against women of color and our communities through direct action, critical dialogue, and grassroots organizing.*

**The Jericho Movement**
National Office
P.O. Box 2164, Chesterfield, VA 23832
nationaljericho@gmail.com • www.thejerichomovement.com

Local chapters in Albuquerque, Baltimore, Chicago, Iowa City, Los
Angeles, New York City, Portland, and Philadelphia.

*The Jericho Movement
grew out of a call for a
national march on the
White House during
Spring Break of 1998 by
political prisoner Jalil
Muntaqim and works
to free U.S. political
prisoners. The Jericho
website contains an
address listing for U.S.
political prisoners.*

**Jonah House: Nonviolence, Community, Resistance**
1301 Moreland Avenue, Baltimore, MD 21216
410-233-6238
www.jonahhouse.org

*Jonah House is a longtime nonviolence resistance community.
The website includes large amounts of information and updates
on Plowshares anti-nuclear and other anti-militarism and anti-war
direct actions, as well as on political prisoners from those movements, including their letters from prison.*

**Legal Services for Prisoners with Children (LSPC)**
1540 Market St., Suite 490
San Francisco, CA 94102
415-255-7036
info@prisonerswithchildren.org • www.prisonerswithchildren.org

*LSPC organizes communities impacted by the criminal justice sys-
tem and advocates to release incarcerated people, to restore human
and civil rights and to reunify families and communities. We build
public awareness of structural racism in policing, the courts and
prison system and advance racial and gender justice in all our work.*

## Malcolm X Grassroots Movement (MXGM)
National office: (toll free) 877-248-6095
www.mxgm.org

Local chapters in Jackson; Birmingham; Oakland; Atlanta; New York; Washington, DC.

*MXGM is an organization of Afrikans in America/New Afrikans whose mission is to defend the human rights of our people and promote self-determination in our community.*

## The Nation Inside
P.O. Box 448, Wilmington, NC 28402
www.nationinside.org

*Nation Inside is a platform that connects and supports people who are building a movement to systematically challenge mass incarceration in the United States.*

## National Boricua Human Rights Network (NBHRN)
2739 W Division St., Chicago, IL 60622
773-342-8023
info@boricuahumanrights.org • www.boricuahumanrights.org

Local chapters in Cleveland, Detroit, New England, New York, Orlando, Philadelphia, San Francisco.

*NBHRN is an organization composed of Puerto Ricans in the U.S. and their supporters that educates and mobilizes the Puerto Rican community, the broader Latin American community, and other people of conscience regarding issues of justice, peace, and human rights. Our priorities include: (1) the decontamination, development, and return of the island of Vieques to its people; (2) the release of the remaining Puerto Rican political prisoners; and (3) an end to the continuing political repression and criminalization of progressive sectors of the Puerto Rican community.*

Oscar Rohena (CC BY 2.0)

**National Day Laborer Organizing Network (NDLON)**
675 S. Park View St., Suite B, Los Angeles, CA 90057
213-380-2201
info@ndlon.org • www.ndlon.org

*NDLON improves the lives of day laborers in the United States. NDLON works to develop leadership, mobilize, and organize day laborers in order to protect and expand their civil, labor, and human rights. Among other areas of work, NDLON has launched a series of campaigns against ICE detention, deportation and raids, and supports Barrio Defense Committees.*

**National Immigrant Youth Alliance (NIYA)**
www.theniya.org

*NIYA is an undocumented youth-led network of grassroots organizations, campus-based student groups and individuals committed to achieving equality for all immigrant youth, regardless of their legal status through education, empowerment, and escalation of direct action tactics.*

**North American Earth Liberation Prisoners Support Network**
naelpsn@mutualaid.org • www.ecoprisoners.org

*The NA–ELPSN is part of the Earth Liberation Prisoners Support Network (ELP), an international network of groups that support people who are accused or convicted of actions taken in defense of the Earth and its inhabitants.*

**The Nuclear Resister**
P.O. Box 43383, Tucson, AZ 85733
520-323-8697 • nukeresister@igc.org • www.nukeresister.org

*Occasional newspaper and website offering information about and support for imprisoned antinuclear and antiwar activists.*

**Project NIA**
773-392-5165 • www.project-nia.org

*Project NIA is an advocacy, organizing, popular education, research, and capacity-building center with the long-term goal of ending youth incarceration.*

**Prison Activist Resource Center**
P.O. Box 70447, Oakland, CA 94612
510-893-4648
info@prisonactivist.org • www.prisonactivist.org
Political prisoner/POW page: www.prisonactivist.org/pps+pows

*PARC is a prison abolitionist group committed to exposing and challenging the institutionalized racism of the prison industrial complex. PARC produces a directory that is free to prisoners upon request and seeks to work in solidarity with prisoners, formerly incarcerated people, and their friends and families.*

**Prison Radio**
P.O. Box 411074, San Francisco, CA 94141
info@prisonradio.org • www.prisonradio.org

*Prison Radio's mission is to challenge mass incarceration and racism by airing the voices of men and women in prison by bringing their voices into the public dialogue on crime and punishment. Prison Radio produces radio essays and commentaries by political prisoners Mumia Abu-Jamal, Herman Wallace and Albert Woodfox of the Angola 3, and Lori Berenson (U.S. solidarity activist imprisoned in Peru), among others.*

**Prisoner Hunger Strike Solidarity Coalition**
510-444-0484
prisonerhungerstrikesolidarity@gmail.com
prisonerhungerstrikesolidarity.wordpress.com

*PHSS is a coalition based in the Bay Area made up of grassroots organizations and community members committed to amplifying the voices of and supporting the prisoners at Pelican Bay and other CA prisons while on hunger strike.*

Rob McBride / Prisoner Hunger Strike Solidarity Coalition

## ProLibertad Freedom Campaign
718-601-4751
prolibertad@hotmail.com • www.prolibertadweb.org
To join listserv: ProLibertad-subscribe@yahoogroups.com

*The ProLibertad Freedom Campaign is an organization composed of individuals and organizations who work together on a broad and unitary basis, accepting differences of ideological and political position, but sharing the responsibility to support the Puerto Rican political prisoners and prisoners of war who have been imprisoned for their political convictions and activities in the cause of Puerto Rico's ongoing struggle for independence and right to self-determination.*

## Resistance in Brooklyn (RnB)
c/o wrl/Meyer, 339 Lafayette St., New York, NY 10012
mmmsrnb@igc.org

*Resistance in Brooklyn is an affinity group that came together in 1992 to combine political action, study, and a sense of community. RnB has been active in a variety of anti-imperialist solidarity work and movements to free U.S. political prisoners.*

## Rosenberg Fund for Children
116 Pleasant St., Suite 348, Easthampton, MA 01027
413-529-0063 • info@rfc.org • www.rfc.org

*The RFC is a foundation that makes grants to aid children in the U.S. whose parents are targeted progressive activists. We also assist youth who themselves have been targeted as a result of their progressive activities.*

## San Francisco Bay View National Black Newspaper
4917 Third St., San Francisco CA 94124
(415) 671-0789 • editor@sfbayview.com • www.sfbayview.com

*Known as the paper that spread the word to the 30,000 prisoners who joined the 2013 California hunger strike, the Bay View welcomes and features articles by prisoners. Subscriptions are $24 a year in stamps or funds. For prisoners without stamps or funds, the paper is available for free when donations to the Prisoners Subscription Fund are sufficient. Write for a free sample. The Bay View also publishes free pen pal ads.*

## Solitary Watch

P.O. Box 11374,
Washington, DC 20008
solitarywatch.com
solitarywatchnews@gmail.com

*Solitary Watch is a web-based project aimed at bringing the widespread use of solitary confinement out of the shadows and into the light of the public square, through a regularly updatded website. Also publishes a quarterly print edition, in a four-page newsletter format, available for download from their website and as hard copies to prisoners and their families and advocates and to non-profit organizations.*

Rob McBride / Prisoner
Hunger Strike Solidarity Coalition

## South Chicago ABC Zine Distro

P.O. Box 721, Homewood, IL 60430
anthonyrayson@hotmail.com

*Publishes and distributes writings by political prisoners, POWs, and politicized social prisoners.*

## Students Against Mass Incarceration (SAMI)

www.sami-national.org

Local chapters at Howard University, Columbia University, Mount Holyoke College, Morgan State University, University of Maryland, Community College of Baltimore County.

*SAMI is a New Afrikan/Black student organization committed to dismantling the prison industrial complex and effectively putting a stop to mass incarceration. SAMI's mission is to raise awareness on campuses and in communities of the prison industrial complex, existence of political prisoners, police brutality, and recidivism. Our vision is the complete abolition of all prisons and freedom for all political prisoners.*

**Supporting Prisoners and Acting for Radical Change (SPARC)**
P.O. Box 52, Richmond, VA 23218
sparc@signalfire.org
facebook.com/SPARCPrarieFire • sparcprariefire.wordpress.com

*SPARC is a Virginia-based organization providing prisoners revolutionary texts for the purpose of conducting studies and building class consciousness while also facilitating transportation to remote prison locations across the state for families of prisoners. SPARC strives to create a revolutionary mass base against the prison system.*

**Sylvia Rivera Law Project (SRLP)**
147 W 24th St., 5th Floor, New York, NY 10011
212-337-8550
info@srlp.org • www.srlp.org

*SRLP is a collective organization working to improve access to respectful and affirming social, health, and legal services for low-income people and people of color who are transgender, intersex, or gender nonconforming. We believe that in order to create meaningful political participation and leadership, we must have access to basic means of survival and safety from violence.*

Daniel Altrows

**Transgender Gender Variant Intersex**
**Justice in Prison Project (TGIP)**
1201 46th Ave, Oakland, CA 94601
510-533-3144
info@tgijp.org • www.tgijp.org

*TGI Justice Project is a group of transgender people—inside and
outside of prison—creating a united family in the struggle for
survival and freedom. We work in collaboration with others to forge
a culture of resistance and resilience to strengthen us for the fight
against imprisonment, police violence, racism, poverty, and societal
pressures. We seek to create a world rooted in self-determination,
freedom of expression, and gender justice.*


**Turning the Tide:**
**Journal of Anti-Racist Action, Research & Education**
c/o ARA, P.O. Box 1055, Culver City, CA 90232
310-495-0299
antiracist.org • antiracistaction_la@yahoo.com
www.aratoronto.org (archive of recent issues)

*Turning the Tide is an independent, grassroots journal of
antiracism, anticolonialism, and anti-imperialism, with frequent
coverage of U.S. political prisoners. One-year subscriptions in the
U.S. (6 bimonthly issues) are $18 for individuals and $28 for institutions or international subscribers (payable to Anti-Racist Action).*


**War Resisters League**
339 Lafayette St., New York, NY 10012
212-228-0450
wrl@warresisters.org • www.warresisters.org

*Founded in 1923 as a secular group committed to nonviolent social
change, WRL has been the leading consistent support organization for over four generations for U.S. draft resisters, registration
resisters, draft evaders fleeing to Canada and elsewhere, and for
active-duty GI military resisters, working closely with the Iraq
Veterans Against the War and against the interweaving of police
and military forces.*

# About the Authors

**Dan Berger** is a scholar, author, and activist. He is the author or editor of *Letters from Young Activists* (2005), *Outlaws of America: The Weather Underground and the Politics of Solidarity* (2006), *The Hidden 1970s: Histories of Radicalism* (2010), *and Captive Nation: Black Prison Organizing During the Civil Rights Era.* He teaches comparative ethnic studies at the University of Washington at Bothell, where he works with the Beyond the Carceral State initiative. Living in Seattle by way of Philadelphia, Berger is also a founding member of Decarcerate PA. For more, see www.danberger.org

**Ruth Wilson Gilmore** is professor of Earth and Environmental Studies at the Graduate Center of the City University of New York where she directs the Center for Place, Culture, and Politics. Author of *Golden Gulag: Prisons, Surplus, Crisis, and Opposition in Globalizing California*, she is also a founding member of the California Prison Moratorium Project, Critical Resistance, Central California Environmental Justice Network, and other organizations.

**dream hampton** is a mother, filmmaker, community organizer, and a co-resister from Detroit. She has written about music, culture, and politics for more than twenty years. Her articles and essays have appeared in *Detroit News*, *Essence*, *Harper's*, the *Village Voice*, and a dozen anthologies.

## ABOUT PM PRESS

PM Press was founded at the end of 2007
by a small collection of folks with decades
of publishing, media, and organizing
experience. PM Press co-conspirators have
published and distributed hundreds of
books, pamphlets, CDs, and DVDs.

Members of PM have founded enduring book fairs, spear-
headed victorious tenant organizing campaigns, and
worked closely with bookstores, academic conferences, and
even rock bands to deliver political and challenging ideas to
all walks of life. We're old enough to know what we're doing
and young enough to know what's at stake.

PM Press is always on the lookout for talented and skilled
volunteers, artists, activists, and writers to work with. If you
have a great idea for a project or can contribute in some
way, please get in touch.

PM Press
P.O. Box 23912
Oakland, CA 94623

www.pmpress.org

## FRIENDS OF PM PRESS

These are indisputably momentous times—the financial system is melting down globally and the Empire is stumbling. Now more than ever there is a vital need for radical ideas. Friends of PM allows you to directly help impact, amplify, and revitalize the discourse and actions of radical writers, filmmakers, and artists. It provides us with a stable foundation from which we can build upon our early successes and provides a much-needed subsidy for the materials that can't necessarily pay their own way. You can help make that happen—and receive every new title automatically delivered to your door once a month—by joining as a Friend of PM Press. And, we'll throw in a free T-shirt when you sign up.

Here are your options:

- **$30 a month** Get all books and pamphlets plus 50% discount on all webstore purchases
- **$40 a month** Get all PM Press releases (including CDs and DVDs) plus 50% discount on all webstore purchases
- **$100 a month** Superstar—Everything plus PM merchandise, free downloads, and 50% discount on all webstore purchases

For those who can't afford $30 or more a month, we're introducing **Sustainer Rates** at $15, $10, and $5. Sustainers get a free PM Press T-shirt and a 50% discount on all purchases from our website.

Your Visa or Mastercard will be billed once a month, until you tell us to stop. Or until our efforts succeed in bringing the revolution around. Or the financial meltdown of Capital makes plastic redundant. Whichever comes first.

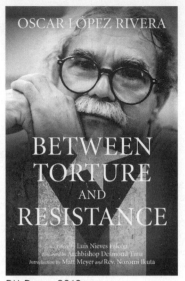

PM Press & Kersplebedeb, 2008
ISBN 9781604860351
912 pages • paperback • $37.95

PM Press, 2013
ISBN 9781604866858
160 pages • paperback • $15.95

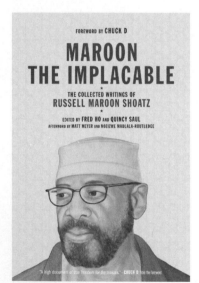

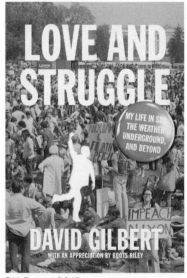

PM Press, 2013
ISBN 9781604860597
312 pages • paperback • $20.00

PM Press, 2012
ISBN 9781604863192
352 pages • paperback • $22.00

PM PRESS, P.O. Box 23912, Oakland, CA 94623
www.pmpress.org

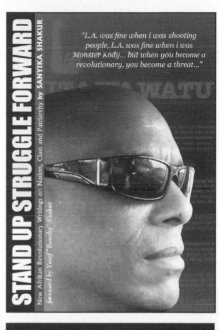
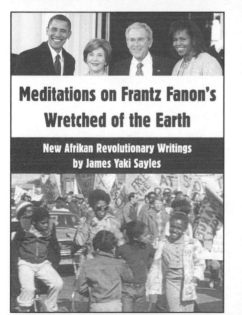

**KER SPL EBE DEB**

Since 1998 Kersplebedeb has been an important source of radical literature and agit prop materials.

The project has a non-exclusive focus on anti-patriarchal and anti-imperialist politics, framed within an anticapitalist perspective. A special priority is given to writings regarding armed struggle in the metropole, and the continuing struggles of political prisoners and prisoners of war.

The Kersplebedeb website provides downloadable activist artwork, as well as historical and contemporary writings by revolutionary thinkers from the anarchist and communist traditions.

Kersplebedeb can be contacted at:

> Kersplebedeb
> CP 63560
> CCCP Van Horne
> Montreal, Quebec
> Canada
> H3W 3H8
>
> email: info@kersplebedeb.com
> web: www.kersplebedeb.com
> secure.leftwingbooks.net

# Kersplebedeb